The New
CIVIL WAR
HANDBOOK

*Facts and Photos
for Readers of All Ages*

Mark Hughes

SB

Cataloging-in-Publication Data is available from the Library of Congress.

ISBN 978-1-932714-62-3

05 04 03 02 01   5 4 3 2 1
First edition, first printing

SB
Published by
Savas Beatie LLC
521 Fifth Avenue, Suite 3400
New York, NY 10175
Phone: 610-853-9131

Editorial Offices:

Savas Beatie LLC
P.O. Box 4527
El Dorado Hills, CA 95762
Phone: 916-941-6896
(E-mail) editorial@savasbeatie.com

Savas Beatie titles are available at special discounts for bulk purchases in the United States by corporations, institutions, and other organizations. For more details, please contact Special Sales, P.O. Box 4527, El Dorado Hills, CA 95762, or you may e-mail us at sales@savasbeatie.com, or visit our website at www.savasbeatie.com for additional information.

To my wife, Patricia (Patty) McDaniel Hughes, and our daughter,
Anna Grace Hughes, without whose support and
encouragement I could not have written this book.

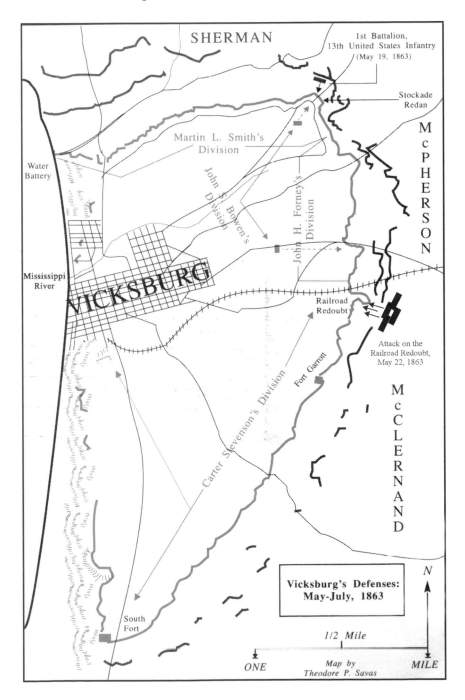

Vicksburg's Defenses:
May-July, 1863

Map by
Theodore P. Savas

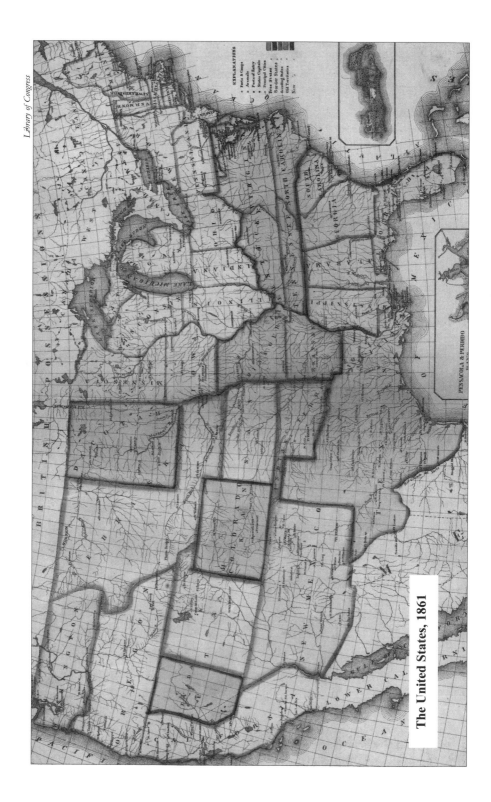

The United States, 1861

Contents

Contents (continued)

Foreword

The first book (really more of a pamphlet) I ever purchased was William Price's *The Civil War Handbook*. I was ten years old, on a visit to the Richmond battlefield with my family, when I spotted a copy in the park's gift shop. The tiny saddle-stitched volume immediately appealed to me. In a mere 60+ pages, the author successfully presented a variety of information—anecdotes, images, and statistics—about the war. It was an instant classic, published at the perfect time: 1961, the first year of the nation's Civil War centennial celebrations.

I've kept my copy of Price's work close at hand over the years. When I started writing books about Civil War cemeteries in the early 1990s, I regularly consulted *The Civil War Handbook* as a quick and easy reference. Although it remains a valuable source, Price's work is woefully outdated. In the nearly 50 years since it was first published, our understanding of the war has changed and expanded. New scholarship has challenged long-held beliefs and previously accepted data, and revealed new avenues of research (the wartime experiences of women and African Americans, for example, are no longer relegated to the historical dustbin). Modern photographic technology has allowed for the restoration and publication of a greater number of Civil War images. And the Internet has opened up countless new opportunities for us to learn about the past, allowing researchers access to vast amounts of digitized archival and genealogical materials.

A few years ago I decided to write my own Civil War handbook, updated and expanded for a 21st century audience. The result you now hold in your hands. *The New Civil War Handbook* contains a wide variety of information on America's greatest conflict. I wanted my book to include material for all levels of Civil War enthusiast: hard data in easy-to-read charts for serious researchers, and lighter fare—from images to anecdotes—for younger or novice buffs. In short, I wanted to do in 2009 what William Price did so well in 1961: create an informative and entertaining Civil War resource for all to use. Only you will know whether I succeeded.

I benefitted from the assistance and encouragement of a number of people as I worked on *The New Civil War Handbook*. My colleagues at Cleveland Community College (Shelby, NC) were particularly helpful: Allen Mosteller, public services / reference librarian at the college's Jim and Patsy Rose Library, located obscure books for me, while library staffers Victoria Linder and Constance Ackley-Staton saved me days of travel by obtaining material through inter-library loan. Barry Boyles, Al Dunkleman, Bruce Mack, Wayne Slocumb, and B.J. Zamora offered support and suggestions. Ron Wright, former vice president of academic programs, encouraged my research (I wish him success with his own writing project) and David Estridge, coordinator of the college's industrial management program, provided his sketch of a minie ball for use in the book.

In my search for Civil War images, I received generous aid from Ms. Jodean Rousey Murdock, museum technician at the Rock Island Arsenal Museum; Mr. Eric N. Blevins, photographer at the North Carolina Museum of History; and Colonel Diane B. Jacob, head of Archives & Records Management at the Virginia Military Institute.

The folks at Savas Beatie made the publication process an enjoyable one. Managing director Ted Savas saw the potential in the project early on. My editor, Terry Johnston, offered many valuable suggestions and helped me develop the structure of this book. Also helpful was Sarah Keeney, Savas Beatie's marketing director.

Special thanks go to Dr. David L. Norris, my mentor at Southeastern Oklahoma State University. Dr. Norris encouraged me to write my first book; this is my fifth. I never would have considered writing without his encouragement.

Finally, my wife, Patricia McDaniel Hughes, and my daughter, Anna Grace Hughes, were invaluable sources of support, generously accompanying me on my many research trips to archives, libraries, cemeteries, and battlefields.

*   *   *

The material presented in *The New Civil War Handbook* was obtained from a variety of sources, the most prominent being: the U.S. War Department's *The War of the Rebellion: A Compilation of the Official Records*; the U.S. Surgeon General Office's *Medical and Surgical History of the War of the Rebellion*; Frederick Dyer's *Compendium of the War of the Rebellion*; Frederick Phisterer's *Statistical Record of the Armies of the United States*; William Fox's *Regimental Losses in the American Civil War, 1861-1865*; and Thomas Livermore's *Numbers and Losses in the Civil War in America, 1861-65*. Unless otherwise noted, all photos are courtesy of the National Archives and Library of Congress.

Publisher's Preface

Why the Civil War, and Why Do We Study it?

There is a simple reason why the Civil War remains popular in books and movies, and why large numbers of tourists visit its battlefields year after year. Except for our founding Revolution, 1861-1865 represents the defining event in our nation's history, and one of the major events in world history.

Bloody war was needed if important constitutional questions were to be settled. The immediate issue revolved around secession. Could a state secede? Was such a thing allowed under the U.S. Constitution, as many believed and openly advocated, or was the act of a state or group of states seeking to leave the Union unconstitutional? Many in the South argued yes. The American Revolution begun in 1775 was not a revolution at all, some explained, but the secession of part of the home country from another segment.

Many people are surprised to learn that it was New England, and not the Southern states, that first raised the specter of secession. States in the Northeast threatened to leave the Union several times, beginning in 1803 when Thomas Jefferson arranged the Louisiana Purchase, again near the end of the War of 1812, and yet a third time more than thirty years later when New England politicians screamed over the annexation of Texas as a slave state.

When South Carolina threatened to withdraw from the Union over economic issues, President Andrew Jackson threatened to invade the state with Federal troops. South Carolina rattled the sword again in 1850, and finally made good on its threats by withdrawing from the Union in December of 1860. The shocking declaration started a landslide that carried several other states with her. War followed in her wake. Only bayonets and bloodshed decided the constitutional issue: the right of secession was not to be found inside the four corners of the Constitution.

Why did Southern states secede? The first eighty years of our existence grounded our original states and those created thereafter in two diametrically opposite philosophical systems: slave and free. Could a country erected on the brick and mortar of individual freedom and self-determination continue with a large percentage of its population in chains? The war decided it could not.

Many reasons were raised then, and are still argued to this day, in an effort to justify separation, from "States' Rights"—and all that entails—to tariff issues, economic matters, and social and cultural differences. Each was a lightening rod for argument and war because each, either directly or indirectly, was tied to the institution of slavery. "[It] is fair to say that had there been no slavery there would have been no war," wrote a prominent Confederate general once the fighting ended. "Slavery was undoubtedly the immediate fomenting cause of the woeful American conflict." The country decided by force of arms that it would no longer tolerate black slavery, and the thread of that decision was spun into our stitched-up Union by way of the 13th, 14th, and 15th amendments to the U.S. Constitution.

In addition to ending human bondage and deciding the right of secession, the war profoundly altered America and its citizens. In the middle 1800s, most men spent their entire lives within a tight radius of their birthplace. But then war came, and young men from Iowa, Minnesota, and Massachusetts enlisted by the tens of thousands in a mad dash to avoid missing what most believed would be a short war. Boys from the rural Iowa prairie found themselves fighting in the swamps of Louisiana; others from big cities marched and died along the Mississippi River; merchants, doctors, clerks, and school teachers, North and South, were blockading Southern ports or manning the massive harbor forts, riding on the roofs of trains through a foreign landscape, or rotting inside prisoner of war camps. Many of those fortunate enough to survive returned home to begin their lives anew. Many others found they were unable to do so, and struck out West to tame new lands and uncover new adventures. All of them, whether they fought for the Union or the Confederacy, began their "second lives" with an entirely different understanding and appreciation for the size and importance of their country, and their own small part in it.

The Civil War devastated most of the Southern states, drained away incalculable wealth, and left a bitterness that lingers to this day. More than 600,000 men died and hundreds of thousands more were injured. In the end, the great American experiment endured. What would the modern world look like if America had been cleaved in half in 1865?

And so I close as I began. There is a reason why the popularity of the Civil War remains strong, why we linger on its fields, why we fight to preserve what is left, and why we endeavor to teach it to our children. If we forget the defining event in our history, the four long years that make us what we are today, we will do so at the peril of our own existence.

Theodore P. Savas
El Dorado Hills, California

SECTION I: FACTS

Naming the War

From the firing upon Fort Sumter down to the present day, dozens of names—neutral, pro-Northern, and pro-Southern—have been assigned to the conflict of 1861 to 1865. While by no means comprehensive, the following list contains, in no particular order, the most popular among them.

The Civil War

The War Between the States

The War of the Rebellion

The Confederate War

The War for Southern Independence

Mr. Lincoln's War

The War of the North and South

The Abolitionists' War

The War of Northern Aggression

The Lost Cause

The Second American Revolution

The Brothers' War

The War of Southern Secession

The Late Unpleasantness

The War for the Union

The War for States' Rights

The War of the Sixties

The Great Rebellion

The Yankee Invasion

The Slaveholders' Rebellion

Civil War Voices

"The art of war is simple enough. Find out where your enemy is. Get at him as soon as you can. Strike him as hard as you can, and keep moving on."

— Ulysses S. Grant

"It's just like shooting squirrels, only these squirrels have guns."

— A veteran Union soldier, instructing new recruits in musket drill.

"We talked the matter over and could have settled the war in thirty minutes had it been left to us."

— Alleged comment of a Confederate soldier after fraternizing with a Union soldier between the lines.

"Look at Jackson's brigade! It stands there like a stone wall!"

— General Barnard E. Bee of South Carolina, describing the performance of fellow Confederate Thomas J. Jackson and his men at the Battle of Bull Run.

"It's bad. It's damned bad."

— Abraham Lincoln, upon hearing of the Union army's defeat at First Bull Run.

"I have seen enough to convince me that this is no war for foreigners. It is our war, and let us cheerfully bear the burden ourselves. . . . We, in the North, send our scum and filth to fight for a reality."

— William Thompson Lusk, 79th New York Infantry.

"I cannot spare this man. He fights!"

— President Abraham Lincoln, when asked to remove Grant from command.

"He lives by the New Testament and fights by the old."

— Historian Douglas S. Freeman's description of Thomas J. "Stonewall" Jackson.

"Press on, press on, men."

— "Stonewall" Jackson's admonishment to his fabled "foot cavalry" on the march.

"I just . . . got there first with the most men."

— Confederate cavalryman and general Nathan Bedford Forrest, explaining his success in battle.

"Tonight we will water our horses in the Tennessee River."

— Confederate General Albert Sidney Johnston, prior to Shiloh, where he was mortally wounded.

"By some strange operation of magic I seem to have become the power of the land."

— George B. McClellan in 1861, shortly after he assumed command of Union forces around Washington.

"It was not war—it was murder."

— Confederate General D.H. Hill, describing their defeat at the Battle of Malvern Hill.

"The Confederate commanders knew no more about the topography of the country than they did about Central Africa. Here was a limited district, the whole of it within a day's march of the city of Richmond, capital of Virginia and the Confederacy, almost the first spot on the continent occupied by the British race, the Chickahominy itself classic by legends of Captain John Smith and Pocahontas; and yet we were profoundly ignorant of the country, were without maps, sketches, or proper guides, and nearly as helpless as if we had been suddenly transferred to the banks of the Lualaba [Congo River]."

— Confederate General Richard Taylor, describing the Confederate high command's ignorance of the terrain during the Seven Days' Battles in 1862.

"I have come to you from the West, where we have always seen the backs of our enemies."

— Union General John Pope, addressing the Army of the Potomac after assuming command. Pope and the army were routed not long thereafter at Second Bull Run.

"Now, if McClellan doesn't want to use the army for awhile, I'd like to borrow it from him and see if I can't do something or other with it."

— Abraham Lincoln, 1862.

"Before this war is over, I intend to be a Major General or a corpse."

Confederate Brigadier General Isaac Trimble, to Stonewall Jackson. Trimble attained the rank and survived the war, minus one leg he lost at Gettysburg.

"It is well that war is so terrible. We should grow too fond of it."

— Robert E. Lee, as he watched the slaughter of Union troops at Fredericksburg.

"General, get up—dress quick—you are a prisoner!"

— Confederate John S. Mosby to Brigadier General Edwin H. Stoughton, whom Mosby awoke with a slap to the rump during a March 1863 nighttime raid on his headquarters.

"The Rebel army is now the legitimate property of the Army of the Potomac."

— Union General Joseph Hooker, shortly before his army's decisive defeat at Chancellorsville.

"Our regt has several recruits imported direct from 'Ould Ireland.' Some of them got into a fight and spent their first night in the guardhouse!"

— Private William Lamson, 20th Maine Infantry.

"All this has been my fault."

— Robert E. Lee, in the wake of the failure of Pickett's Charge at Gettysburg.

"That old man . . . had my division massacred at Gettysburg!"

— George Pickett, to fellow former Confederate officer John S. Mosby, shortly after they paid a postwar visit to Robert E. Lee.

"Well, it made you famous."

— Mosby's rejoinder to Pickett.

"If you don't have my army supplied, and keep it supplied, we'll eat your mules up, sir."

— William T. Sherman, to an army quartermaster before moving his army from Chattanooga toward Atlanta.

"They woke us up before dawn and lined us up in the woods. We didn't get any breakfast. The Yankees fired too high. By night I was covered in green leaves the Yankee bullets had cut off the trees."

— Private Andrew Jackson Hughes, Co. E, 12th North Carolina Infantry, describing the Battle of the Wilderness to his young grandson.

"They couldn't hit an elephant at this distance."

— Union General John Sedgwick, moments before a Confederate sniper killed him at Spotsylvania Court House in May 1864.

"I shall come out of this fight a live major general or a dead brigadier."

— Confederate Brigadier General Albert Perrin, on the eve of the Battle of Spotsylvania, where he was killed.

"Turn my face to the enemy."

— Union General James Clay Rice to his surgeon, after the latter amputated the mortally wounded Rice's leg at a Spotsylvania Court House field hospital.

"I propose to fight it out on this line if it takes all summer."

— Ulysses S. Grant, May 9, 1864, from Spotsylvania Court House.

"The dead covered more than five acres . . . about as thickly as they could be laid."

— A veteran Confederate soldier, describing the carnage after the Battle of Cold Harbor.

"We have five times as many generals here as we want, but are greatly in need of privates. Anyone volunteering in that capacity will be thankfully received."

— Henry Halleck, chief of staff of the U.S. Army, as a Confederate force approached Washington D.C. in 1864.

"On the authority of Lord God Almighty, have you anything that outranks that?"

— "Mother" Mary Ann Ball Bickerdyke, Union army nurse, to a U.S. Army surgeon who questioned the authority upon which she acted.

"War is cruelty. There is no use trying to reform it. The crueler it is, the sooner it will be over."

— Union General William Tecumseh Sherman

"I have been up to see the [CSA] Congress and they do not seem to be able to do anything except to eat peanuts and chew tobacco, while my army is starving."

— General Robert E. Lee

"I saw at a glance where the feeling of England was. They hoped for our ruin! They are jealous of our power. They care neither for the South nor the North. They hate both."

— Cassius Clay, U.S. Minister to Russia.

"General, unless he offers us honorable terms, come back and let us fight it out!"

— Confederate General James Longstreet to Robert E. Lee, as Lee departed to discuss terms for surrender with Grant.

"Any man who is in favor of a further prosecution of this war is a fit subject for a lunatic asylum, and ought to be sent there immediately."

— Nathan Bedford Forrest, May 1865.

"I found afterward that 500 of my men were left dead and wounded on a line as straight as a dress parade."

— Brigadier General Alfred Iverson, CSA, describing the carnage of the Battle of Gettysburg's first day.

"My people are going to war. They are in dead earnest, believing it to be for liberty."

— Confederate officer E.P. Alexander on his reason for resigning from the U.S. Army.

"The Rebel bullet that can kill me has not yet been molded."

— Philip Kearny, a fighting Union one-armed general who was shot and killed at Chantilly, Virginia, in 1862.

"The American people and the Government at Washington may refuse to recognize it for a time; but the 'inexorable logic of events' will force it upon them in the end; that the war now being waged in this land is a war for and against slavery; and that it can never be effectually put down till one or the other of these vital forces is completely destroyed."

— Frederick Douglass, 1861.

"If the Confederacy falls, there should be written on its tombstone, 'Died of a theory.'"

— Confederate President Jefferson Davis.

"You cannot make soldiers of slaves, or slaves of soldiers. The day you make a soldier of them is the beginning of the end of the revolution. And if slaves seem good soldiers, then our whole theory of slavery is wrong."

— Confederate General Howell Cobb, a former U.S. Congressman, on Robert E. Lee's late- war proposal of enlisting slaves in the Confederate army.

"Strange as it may seem to you, but the more men I saw killed the more reckless I became."

— Union soldier Franklin H. Bailey in a letter to his parents.

"The first thing in the morning is drill, drill, a little more drill. Then drill, and lastly drill. Between drills we drill, and sometimes stop to eat a little and have a roll-call."

— Private Oliver Wilcox Norton, 83rd Pennsylvania Volunteers, in 1861.

"The great fact which we asserted from the first is now placed beyond reach of controversy. We said the North could never subdue the South, and the North has now proclaimed the same conclusion."

— *The Times* (London), September 14, 1864.

"The rebel position was unassailable; it was a perfect slaughter-pen, and column after column was broken against it. Our artillery did so little injury to the enemy that they were able to concentrate all their fire on the advancing columns of troops. Besides, an oblique flank fire swept us, so that whole regiments melted away before it."

— Lt. Daniel George Macnamara, 9th Massachusetts Volunteers, describing the carnage at Fredericksburg.

"But hardtack was not so bad an article of food, even when traversed by insects, as may be supposed. Eaten in the dark, no one could tell the difference between it and hardtack that was untenanted."

— John D. Billings, 10th Massachusetts Battery.

"The premonitions that men have before going into battle are very curious and interesting, particularly when they come true. We had on board the *Powhatan* a fine young seaman named Flannigan, who came from Philadelphia. On the night of the 14th of January he came to my room with a small box in his hand, and said to me, 'Mr. Evans, will you be kind enough to take charge of this box for me—it has some little trinkets in it—and give it to my sister in Philadelphia?' I asked him why he did not deliver it himself, to which he replied, 'I am going ashore with you to-morrow, and will be killed'."

— Ensign Robley D. Evans, US Navy. Seaman Flannigan was killed in the Federal attack on Fort Fisher, North Carolina.

"I spent most of this day with the Yankee wounded. They were in miserable condition. . . . . I heard their confessions, anointed some . . . and aided in washing and dressing some (of their wounds)."

— Rev. James B. Sheeran, Chaplain, 14th Louisiana, CSA.

"The deaths yesterday (September 20, 1864) were twenty-nine. Air pure, location healthy, no epidemic. The men are being deliberately murdered by the surgeon, especially by the ignorance or the malice of the chief."

— A. M. Keiley, a member of the Virginia House of Delegates, who kept the "Dooms-Day" Book (roster of Confederate POW's) at the Elmira (NY) prisoner of war camp.

"[His is] a utterly hopeless case. . . . All you can do is to help him die easy."

— A Union surgeon to Mary Ashton Rice Livermore, a volunteer nurse in the Union Hospital at St. Louis.

"I used to belong to the Methodist church, but I fell away. Oh, send for a Methodist minister!"

— A dying Union soldier to Mary Ashton Rice Livermore, a volunteer nurse in the Union Hospital at St. Louis.

"No, but he found me!"

— Union General Samuel Davis Sturgis after his defeat at Battle of Brice's Crossroads on June 10, 1864, in reply to a woman who asked him, "General, did you find General Forrest?"

"I have no command. They were all killed."

— Brigadier General Abraham Buford, after the Southern defeat at Tupelo, Mississippi.

"Let them go. They can take any thing they find, and do any thing they want, except take the chair I am sitting in."

— Col. Edward Hatch, USA, refusing the pleas of Mrs. Jacob Thompson to stop his men from looting her house, Memphis 1864.

"When daylight dawned on Franklin, Tenn., December 1, 1864, the scene was indescribable. About five thousand Confederates and two thousand Federals lay dead or wounded in and around the Federal breast-works. In many instances, Confederates and Federals lay across each other, and there was one case where a Confederate and a Federal were found dead in the ditch, the Confederate grasping the Federal's throat."

— Lt. James Dinkins, Company C, 18th Mississippi Infantry.

"It's hard to die here. I had hoped to die at home."

— Pvt. D. S. Birdsell, Company C, 16th Connecticut, who died at Andersonville prison.

"The only son of his mother and she was a widow."

— Inscription on the tombstone of Confederate Brigadier General Samuel Garland, Jr., killed in the Battle of South Mountain.

"Each of them [barns] was a field hospital; its floor covered with mutilated soldiers, and surgeons busy at the lantern-lighted operating tables. By the door of one of them was a ghastly pile of amputated arms and legs, and around each of them lay multitudes of wounded men, covering the ground by the acre, wrapped in their blankets and awaiting their turns under the knife. I was stopped hundreds of times by wounded men, sometimes accompanied by a comrade but often wandering alone, to be asked in faint tones the way to the hospital of their division, till the accumulated sense of the bloodshed and suffering of the day became absolutely appalling. It seemed to me as if every square yard of the ground, for many square miles, must have its blood stain."

— Lt. George Benedict, 12th Vermont, describing the night after the Battle of Antietam.

"Then write to my mother and father that I tried to do my duty."

— 16-year-old Private James Sullivan, Company K, 21st Massachusetts, after a surgeon told his sergeant, "He can't last five minutes."

"He said that he had called for help . . . a prowling rascal had turned him over and taken his watch."

— Charles Walcott, 21st Massachusetts, describing his encounter with a mortally wounded Confederate officer the night after the battle of Antietam.

"Every man's pocket was turned inside out . . . every one was robbed by the ghouls."

— Private J. Polk Racine, 5th Maryland Infantry [Federal], describing the robbing of battlefield dead.

"The Revolution (Civil War) is raging at all points while the folly, weakness, and criminality of our heads (leaders) is becoming more decidedly manifest. Abraham Lincoln has neither sense or principle. McClellan is a capital soldier but has no capacity to take political lead. The people are strong and willing but 'there is no king in Israel.' The man of the day has not yet come."

– Lt. Col. David Hunter Strother on September 24, 1862. Strother was on McClellan's staff during the Antietam Campaign.

"Eventual victory must be yours, as far as man can judge. But at how terrible a cost? Look this well in the face! That of extermination. . . . Let the South go."

— Archer Gurney, Paris, France, in a May 24, 1861, letter to the editor, New York *Times*.

"The wound was a compound fracture of the upper third of my right thigh. I was taken to Hood's division hospital, on John Plank's farm, where was a surgeon of the Eleventh Georgia. They carried me to a tent, but said it was no use, I would certainly die. They ordered me to the dead-house, where I remained fifteen days."

— Captain O. H. Miller, of Georgia, wounded at Gettysburg on July 2, 1862. Miller survived the war, but his right leg was 4 ½ inches shorter than his left.

Did You Know?
Interesting Facts About the Civil War

Four of First Lady Mary Todd Lincoln's brothers and two of her brothers-in-law served in the Confederate army.

The first federal income tax was levied in 1862 to help finance the war.

The average age of Union soldiers at time of enlistment was 25.8 years.

Of the 1,080 officers in the United States Army at the outbreak of the war, 313 (almost 29%) resigned and joined the Confederate military. U.S. Army enlisted men were much more loyal: only 26 out of some 15,000 switched allegiances.

In 1861, a private in the Union army earned $13.00 a month. A Union brigadier general received $315.00 a month.

Privates in Confederate infantry and artillery units earned $11.00 a month in 1861. Confederate brigadier generals drew $301.00 a month.

In one of the several documented cases of brother facing brother in combat during the war, Confederate Franklin Buchanan commanded the CSS *Virginia* (aka *Merrimac*) in an attack on the USS *Congress*, during which his brother, McKeen, on board the *Congress*, was killed.

Though many brothers died fighting for opposite sides, the Terrill brothers of Virginia were the only two to do so as generals: Union Brigadier General William Rufus Terrill was killed at the Battle of Perryville, Kentucky, in October 1862, while his brother, Confederate Brigadier General James Barbour Terrill, was killed in action near Bethesda Church, Virginia, in 1864.

According to an 1879 estimate, the United States spent $6,190,000,000 on the war.

John L. Clem, "the Drummer Boy of Chickamauga," enlisted in the Union army when he was 10 years old. In 1915, he earned the distinction as the last Civil War veteran to retire from the U.S. Army.

On October 27, 1864, Joseph Banks Lyle, a captain in the 5th South Carolina Infantry, single-handedly captured over 600 Union soldiers with an unloaded rifle.

Approximately one of every four Union soldiers was born outside the United States. Of immigrants who served, Germans formed the largest group, followed by the Irish.

Confederate Partisan Raider John S. Mosby, known as "The Grey Ghost," disbanded his command at war's end rather than surrender to U.S. authorities. Mosby later angered his former comrades by supporting Ulysses S. Grant during his run for the presidency in 1868.

At Gettysburg, the 1st Minnesota Infantry suffered the highest percentage of casualties in a single engagement of any U.S. unit: by battle's end, 215 (82%) of its 262 men were killed, wounded, or missing.

At Sharpsburg (Antietam), the 1st Texas Infantry had 186 of its 226 men (82.3%) killed, wounded, or missing.

Thirteen men named Abraham Lincoln served in the Union army. One served in the Confederacy, as a member of the 1st Squadron, Cherokee Mounted Volunteers.

Forty-four men named Jefferson Davis served in the Union army. One, Jefferson C. Davis, rose to the rank of brevet major general.

William H. Carney, a former slave who served as a sergeant in the 54th Massachusetts Infantry, was the first African American awarded the Congressional Medal of Honor, for his actions at Fort Wagner, South Carolina, on July 18, 1863.

Nearly half (49 percent) of Union soldiers worked in agricultural jobs at their time of enlistment. Less than one percent were printers.

The only civilian casualty of the Battle of Gettysburg was a young woman, Mary Virginia "Jennie" Wade, who was shot and killed by an errant bullet while making bread in her sister's house.

According to astronomer Benjamin Gould, whose comprehensive *Investigations in the Military and Anthropological Statistics of American Soldiers* was published in 1869, the tallest documented Union soldier was a lieutenant in the 27th Indiana Infantry, who measured 82 1/2 inches (nearly 6 feet, 11 inches) in his stocking feet. The shortest documented Union soldier was a 24-year-old enlistee in the 192nd Ohio Infantry who measured but 40 inches tall (3 feet, 3 1/3 inches).

Despite the dire threats of both commissioned and non-commissioned officers, no Union soldier was executed for falling asleep while on guard duty.

The Confederacy won both the first (Fort Sumter, South Carolina, April 12-14, 1861) and last (Palmito Ranch, Texas, May 12-13, 1865) battles of the war.

Albert Woolson, the last recognized surviving Union soldier, died in 1956.

*   *   *

What's in a Name?

Most Civil War battles were known by more than one name. Union commanders tended to name a battle after the nearest river, stream, or creek. Hence, the Northern name for the war's first major land battle (fought around Manassas, Virginia) was named after Bull Run, the creek that flowed between the armies. Confederates, however, tended to name battles after the nearest city or town. Thus, Confederates referred to the war's first major land battle as Manassas. The major battle of Antietam (named after the creek) was referred to as Sharpsburg (after the small town). One of the few major battles that everyone called by the same name was . . . Gettysburg.

Civil War Veterans Better Known
for Other Achievements

While many Civil War soldiers and civilians achieved fame as a result of their actions during the conflict, others rose to prominence well after the guns fell silent:

Steamboat pilot Samuel Longhorne Clemens helped form a Confederate Militia unit in his native Missouri at the beginning of the war. The company soon disbanded, and Clemens struck out west to mine silver in Nevada. Soon thereafter, he began writing stories based on the adventures of his early life. By the time of his death in 1910, Clemens—better known by his pen name, Mark Twain—had earned a reputation as one of America's great authors.

As a teenager, George Westinghouse served in both the Union army and navy. His experiences as an engineering officer aboard a steam-powered warship apparently helped [set] loose his creativity—Westinghouse went on to a prolific career as an inventor and entrepreneur. A rival of Thomas Edison, Westinghouse patented over 400 inventions—including the railroad air brake—before his death.

Indiana native Lew Wallace led the Union army at the Battle of Monocacy, Maryland, in the summer of 1864. After the war, the former major general served as governor of New Mexico Territory and U.S. minister to the Ottoman Empire. Despite these accomplishments, Wallace earned his fame as an author: his 1880 novel, *Ben Hur*, remains in print to this day.

Welsh immigrant Henry Morton Stanley reluctantly served as a private in the 6th Arkansas Infantry. He was captured at Shiloh, sent to Chicago's Camp Douglas, and enlisted in the Union army. A newspaper correspondent after the war, Stanley was dispatched to Africa in 1871 to search for missing Scottish missionary David Livingstone. Upon finding him, Stanley is said to have uttered the famed line, "Dr. Livingstone, I presume?"

A member of the Confederate signal corps, Sidney Lanier was captured while serving aboard a blockade-runner and spent three months in the prison camp at Point Lookout, Maryland. Lanier survived the war to become a prolific poet and musician, but the tuberculosis he contracted while a prisoner weakened his health, and he died in 1881 at age 39.

Union soldier Rutherford B. Hayes was wounded at the Battle of South Mountain in 1862. Elected president of the United States in 1876, Hayes soon thereafter removed the last Federal soldiers occupying the southern states.

William McKinley was an 18-year-old teacher in a small Ohio school when he enlisted as a private in the Union army in 1861. Thirty-five years later, McKinley was elected the twenty-fifth president of the United States, the last of six Union veterans to rise to the position.

John Jacob Astor III served as an aide-de-camp on General George McClellan's staff during the Peninsular Campaign and was brevetted brigadier general of volunteers. Astor, grandson of the millionaire fur trader, enjoyed a life of luxury after the war.

Louisa May Alcott's service as a nurse in a Union hospital in Georgetown, Virginia, almost killed her—she contacted typhoid fever, and the drug used to treat her weakened her heart. She went on to a career as a novelist, and is best known for her work *Little Women*, based partly on her family's experiences during the conflict.

In 1862, Indianapolis resident Eli Lilly organized the 18th Battery, Indiana Light Artillery. Though Lilly, a pharmacist by trade, had no formal military training, he proved to be a competent leader, rising to the rank of colonel. After the war, Lilly founded a small pharmaceutical company that grew into the Eli Lilly and Company, which today stands as one of the world's largest corporations.

Henry Algernon du Pont, an 1861 graduate of West Point, received the Congressional Medal of Honor for his actions at the Battle of Cedar Creek, Virginia. Colonel du Pont remained in the army for ten years after the war before becoming an executive with the family chemical company.

Du Pont refused its presidency to instead run for the U.S. Senate, to which he was elected in 1906.

As a teenager, Jesse James joined his brother Frank in serving with bands of Confederate guerrillas who operated in the Deep South ambushing Union troops. After the war, James used some of the tactics he learned in his career as an outlaw; he and his gang allegedly pulled off the first daylight bank robbery in American history.

One author closely associated with the Civil War never fought in it. The vivid descriptions of combat and soldiering in Stephen Crane's 1895 book *The Red Badge of Courage: An Episode of the American Civil War* led many readers to assume that the author had served during the war. But Crane was born in 1871, six years after it ended.

Organization of the Armies

These graphics provide a general representation of the organization of Union and Confederate armies. Armies consisted of multiple corps (pronounced "core"), which in turn consisted of two or more divisions. Whereas Confederate regiments were generally organized in the same way as their Union counterparts, Confederate corps (as shown) contained more component parts than Union corps, and so were larger. (For example, the Army of Northern Virginia consisted of three corps, the Army of the Potomac double that.) U.S. policy created new regiments to accommodate new recruits, unlike the Confederacy, which sent replacement troops to existing regiments.

UNITED STATES ARMY*

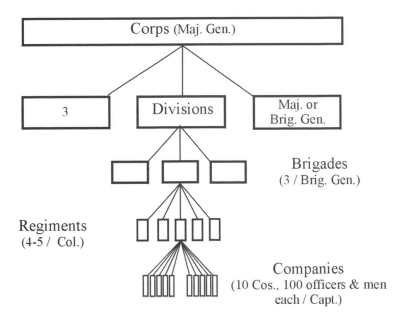

* This organization is intended as a general guide only. In practice, the organization of armies and the ranks of commanders varied widely. For example, some corps had as few as two divisions, some divisions as few as two brigades, and many colonels commanded brigades in the field. These are but a few examples of how this structure varied in practice.

CONFEDERATE STATES ARMY*

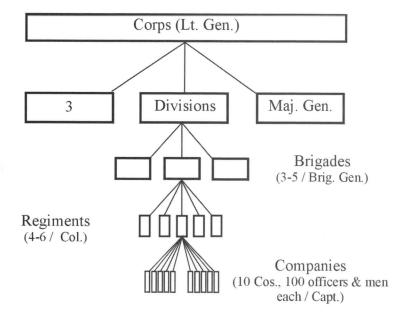

* This organization is intended as a general guide only. In practice, the organization of armies and the ranks of commanders varied widely. For example, some corps had as few as two divisions, some divisions as few as two brigades, and many colonels commanded brigades in the field. These are but a few examples of how this structure varied in practice.

SECTION 2: IMAGES OF WAR

Civil War Begins

Jefferson Davis enjoyed a distinguished career as an officer in the Mexican War and served as Secretary of War under President Franklin Pierce. As a senator from Mississippi, he was not among those who urged secession. Although he expected to play a military role in the Civil War, he reluctantly accepted the presidency of the Confederate States of America.

Abraham Lincoln, a native of Kentucky, was a lawyer and congressman before the Civil War. In 1860, he was elected as the sixteenth president of the United States of America. He frequently used jokes and varying forms of humor to make important points.

The bombardment of Fort Sumter (top) on April 12, 1861, and the interior of the fort (bottom) following its surrender on April 14.

Generals

After his home state of Virginia seceded from the Union in April 1861, career soldier **Robert E. Lee** resigned from the U.S. Army to fight for the Confederacy. An excellent strategist who was revered by his men, Lee took command of the Army of Northern Virginia in June 1862 and led it to a string of victories against larger enemy armies. Forced on the defensive in 1864, he surrendered at Appomattox in April 1865.

West Point graduate **Ulysses Simpson Grant** entered the war as a captain and emerged as the Union's greatest commander. After gaining fame for his victories in the war's Western Theater, Grant was promoted to general-in-chief of the entire U.S. Army in 1864 and headed to the Eastern Theater to face Lee and his Army of Northern Virginia. He battled Lee almost nonstop, from the moment he plunged into the Wilderness in May 1864 until Appomattox in April 1865.

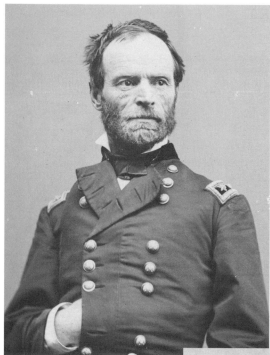

As a commander, Grant's friend and loyal subordinate **William Tecumseh Sherman** was both able and controversial. His long campaign of maneuver and fighting from North Georgia to Atlanta captured that important city in September 1864. Atlanta's fall helped make possible President Lincoln's reelection that fall. Sherman's infamous "March to the Sea" introduced what some historians describe as "total warfare" to the Southern population.

Joseph E. Johnston led Confederate troops in the first major battle of the Civil War (Manassas, or Bull Run) and the last battle (Bentonville, North Carolina). When he was severely wounded at Seven Pines in May 1862, Old Joe was replaced by Robert E. Lee. Johnston returned to army command and skillfully opposed Sherman across North Georgia in the Atlanta campaign and later fighting in the Carolinas. When Sherman died in 1891, the 84-year-old Joe Johnston marched hatless during his funeral procession under a heavy, cold rain. He developed pneumonia and died less than five weeks later.

Virginian **Thomas Jonathan Jackson** may have struggled as a student at West Point, but he thrived on the battlefield. His steady performance at First Manassas earned him the nickname "Stonewall," and his exploits during the Shenandoah Valley Campaign of 1862 brought him iconic status in the young Confederacy. His career and life were cut short at Chancellorsville, where he was mortally wounded by friendly fire.

Hailed as a "Young Napoleon" at the beginning of the war, **George Brinton McClellan** proved to be an excellent army administrator. However, as a commander he was gripped by an excessive sense of caution, which contributed to his defeat by General Lee in the Seven Days Battles outside Richmond. Similar caution prevented McClellan from crushing Lee's outnumbered army a second time at Antietam in Maryland in September 1862. Relieved of command by Lincoln that fall, McClellan ran against the president in the 1864 election and lost decisively, carrying only three states.

James Ewell Brown "JEB" Stuart's classmates at West Point mockingly called him "Beauty." Among the most famous cavalry commanders of the war, Stuart was known for his chivalry and audacity. During one of his several raids into the North, he telegraphed Union Quartermaster General Montgomery Meigs to complain about the U.S. mules his raiders had seized—their quality was such that they were slowing the removal of the wagons he had captured! Stuart was killed in the fighting at Yellow Tavern in May 1864.

Although he graduated dead last in his class at West Point, **George Armstrong Custer** quickly earned a reputation as a dynamic cavalryman among the press and his superiors in the army. He fought with a fearlessness bordering on recklessness (he had eleven horses killed under him during the Civil War), and expected no less from the men who served under him. When he was killed at Little Big Horn in 1876, Custer was only 36 years old.

Joseph Hooker was Lincoln's choice to replace Ambrose Burnside as commander of the Army of the Potomac after the debacle at Fredericksburg in late 1862. Hooker, dubbed "Fighting Joe" by the press, was popular with his men but was no match for Robert E. Lee, who outgeneraled the Massachusetts native at Chancellorsville in early May 1863. Hooker asked to be relieved of command on the eve of the battle of Gettysburg, and Lincoln agreed. Hooker fought well as a corps commander in the Western Theater in 1864.

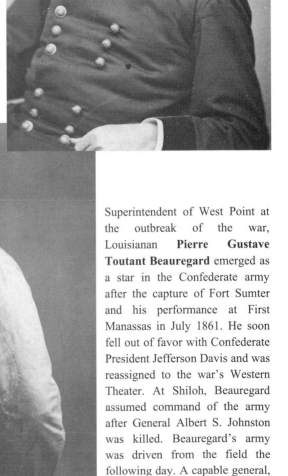

Superintendent of West Point at the outbreak of the war, Louisianan **Pierre Gustave Toutant Beauregard** emerged as a star in the Confederate army after the capture of Fort Sumter and his performance at First Manassas in July 1861. He soon fell out of favor with Confederate President Jefferson Davis and was reassigned to the war's Western Theater. At Shiloh, Beauregard assumed command of the army after General Albert S. Johnston was killed. Beauregard's army was driven from the field the following day. A capable general, Beauregard never lived up to his abilities.

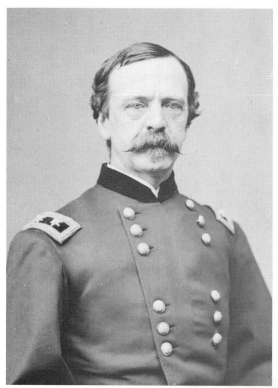

On the second day of the Battle of Gettysburg, **Daniel Sickles** moved his Third Corps forward without orders to higher ground, where James Longstreet's Confederates attacked it in some of the war's most intense fighting. The enemy attack decimated General Sickles' command and cost him a leg. After the war, Sickles spearheaded the campaign to preserve Gettysburg as a national park. It was that move, and not anything he did on the field, that is his real lasting legacy to America.

Friends called **James Longstreet** "Old Pete," a name given to him as a boy by his father. Robert E. Lee referred to Longstreet as his "Old War Horse" after the latter's sterling performance at Sharpsburg in 1862. Longstreet led the Army of Northern Virginia's First Corps through many of the war's most trying battles, including the Seven Days Battles, Second Manassas, Fredericksburg, and Gettysburg. He was critically wounded by his men in the Wilderness in May 1864. After the war, he became a Republican, the party of his friend and former adversary U.S. Grant, provoking the ire of many Southerners.

William S. Rosecrans' star rose steadily in the war's Western Theater when he beat his Confederate opponents at Corinth, Stones River, and outmaneuvered them in the Tullahoma Campaign. Unfortunately, a poorly worded order at Chickamauga in North Georgia on September 20, 1863, left a gaping hole in his line, through which James Longstreet's Confederates poured, driving his Army of the Cumberland from the field. The Chickamauga defeat effectively ended his Civil War career.

Braxton Bragg commanded the luckless Confederate Army of Tennessee in a series of battles, including Perryville, Stones River, Tullahoma, Chickamauga, and the Chattanooga Campaign. His army won its only clear-cut victory of the war at Chickamauga; at Chattanooga, Bragg's army was driven into Georgia in a decisive defeat that finally led to his removal. Bragg's very difficult personality and grating manner created dissension and turmoil within his own ranks. He was President Jefferson Davis' loyal friend, however, and Davis repaid him by keeping him in command far longer than was prudent.

John Sedgwick was a professional soldier, and his father was a general in the American Revolution. He turned in a solid performance during the Peninsula Campaign in the spring of 1862, and his division was nearly trapped and annihilated at Antietam later that fall. In May 1864, at Spotsylvania Court House, his aides cautioned Sedgwick to be wary of Rebel sharpshooters. The general dismissed them with a laugh: "They couldn't hit an elephant at this distance." Within moments, a well-aimed sniper's bullet struck Sedgwick just below the left eye, killing him instantly.

Patrick Cleburne, a native of County Cork, Ireland, earned a well-deserved reputation as an outstanding combat general at the head of a brigade and later, a division. His star dimmed when he urged his fellow officers of the Army of Tennessee to join his call for slaves to be freed to fight as Confederate soldiers. The idea was met with hostility and dismissed by Jefferson Davis. The "Stonewall of the West" was one of five Confederate generals killed at Franklin, Tennessee, in November 1864.

Soldiers

Many new soldiers had their photographs taken to send home as keepsakes for family and friends. This young recruit (top) was from Ohio.

George Green (right) served as a corporal in the 42nd North Carolina Infantry. He was wounded on May 31, 1862, at Seven Pines in Virginia. In 1864, he died in a Richmond hospital. When he heard the sad news, George's father traveled to Richmond to bring his son's body back to North Carolina for burial.
Sandra H. Dill-Little

Edwin Francis Jemison of the 2nd Louisiana (bottom right) was among the war's early volunteers. The 17-year-old was killed at Malvern Hill in July 1862.

One of the estimated 219,000 Confederates who died during the war. All that is known about North Carolina volunteer Jim Costner (below) is written on the back of his picture: "Ma Ma Sanders's uncle—killed in the Confederate War." *Terry Bowen*

One of the estimated 360,000 Union soldiers who died as a result of the war. John Kinsella (above) was 14 when he lied about his age and joined Company C, 7th Connecticut Infantry as a drummer. Captured at Bermuda Hundred, Virginia, he survived the horrors of Andersonville prison only to die on his way home.

Walter C. Jones' New Testament saved his life twice. A private in the 8th New York Cavalry, he carried the book in his shirt pocket. The little volume deflected Confederate minie balls meant for him at Cedar Creek and again at Appomattox Court House.

A young private of the 4th Michigan Infantry (left) strikes a distinctly unmilitary pose for the camera. Western troops often appeared less "polished" than their Eastern counterparts. Note his large Bowie knife and plaid shirt.

West Point cadet John Meigs, (right) the son of U.S. Quartermaster General Montgomery Meigs, graduated first in his class in 1863. John was killed the following year while trying to elude a Confederate patrol in the Shenandoah Valley. Thinking that bushwhackers killed him, General Phillip Sheridan ordered homes within a five-mile radius of Dayton, Virginia, burned to the ground in retaliation.

Andrew Jackson Hughes (right) joined the Cleveland Guards, the first Confederate unit raised in Cleveland County, North Carolina, one week after the outbreak of the war. He would spend time as a prisoner of war and be wounded twice before its end. In 1923, Hughes' son was awarded the Pulitzer Prize for drama. His great-great-grandson is the author of this book.

Jaqueline Beverly Stanard (left) was 18 when he entered the Virginia Military Institute (VMI). In less than a year and a half he was dead, killed in battle at New Market, Virginia. *Virginia Military Institute Archives*

Joseph White Latimer (right) dropped out of VMI to join the Confederate army in 1861. Promoted in 1863, the "Boy Major" was directing his battery at Gettysburg when a fragment from a Union artillery shell struck his leg. Amputation did not save him; the young officer died less than a month shy of his 20th birthday. *Virginia Military Institute Archives*

Moses Ezekiel, 19, fought alongside his fellow VMI cadets at the Battle of New Market. After the war, he moved to Europe and became a world famous sculptor. Ezekiel is buried in Arlington National Cemetery next to the Confederate Monument, the sculpture he regarded as his masterpiece. *Virginia Military Institute Archives*

John Thomas Ellis left his post as the commissioner of revenue in Amherst County, Virginia, to enlist in the Confederate army. Wounded in the thigh at Gaines' Mill, he was promoted to lieutenant colonel in September 1862. At Gettysburg, Ellis was decapitated by a cannon ball during the prolonged artillery duel preceding Pickett's Charge. *Virginia Military Institute Archives*

(Left) Confederate Robert Patterson, a private in Company D, 12th Tennessee Infantry, poses for a camera dressed in a dark blue-gray frock. His right hand grips a single-shot pistol. A bone-handled Bowie knife is tucked into his waist belt. The 12th Tennessee lost heavily in the fighting at the Stones River (Murfreesboro) on December 31, 1862, to January 2, 1863. Patterson was wounded during the combat, lingered for a few days, and died in a hospital.

Four Union Michigan Zouaves pose with 1842 model muskets. Some Union and Confederate regiments dressed soldiers in colorful Zouave-like attire, inspired by French army units of the same name. Although these Michiganders do not have the baggy trousers typical of many Zouave uniforms, they do sport Zouave tasseled fezzes and white canvas leggings. Note the two middle soldiers are smoking cigars.

A Soldier's Life

Members of a Union regiment with bayonets fixed (top) march along a road near their camp outside Washington, D.C. Soldiers on both sides spent countless hours learning the complex movements necessary for survival on a Civil War battlefield. (Bottom) During the warmer months, soldiers lived in tents. A poorly located or ill-constructed camp could lead to serious troubles. Heavy rain might turn an area into a muddy quagmire, and improper sanitation often led to disease, which killed twice as many soldiers as bullets.

(Top) During the winter months, armies abandoned their tents for more substantial quarters like these, built by Southerners near Manassas, Virginia, in 1861.

(Above) When not on duty, men occupied their time a variety of different ways, including liquid refreshment during a game of cards.

(Right) Not all soldiers spent their free time engaged in vice or frivolity. Engineers from the 50th New York constructed this chapel during the siege of Petersburg.

Sundays brought less drill and a chance for worship. This 1861 photograph shows Chaplain Thomas H. Mooney conducting a religious service for New York soldiers, a scene repeated countless times throughout the camps on both sides.

Noncommissioned officers of the 93rd New York gather for food and refreshment. The majority of Civil War soldiers rarely ate so well—or in such style.

(Top) Soldiers augmented their rations by purchasing items from sutlers, operators of mobile stores who traveled from camp to camp. Sutlers offered a variety of goods for sale, including food, tobacco, and drink. (Bottom) Not every soldier carried a gun. Members of the Elmira Cornet Band, 33rd New York Infantry, posed for this photograph in July 1861.

(Top) Five men from the Union Irish Brigade in 1862. Two are Catholic chaplains: James M. Dillon of the 63rd New York (seated, center) and the more widely recognized William Corby of the 88th New York (seated, right). (Bottom) Both Union and Confederate armies took measures to ensure discipline and order. Punishments were based on the severity of the crime. This Union soldier, found guilty of thievery, is shown being drummed out of camp. Soldiers who were found guilty of desertion faced the possibility of execution.

Battles and Battlefields

(Top) A combat image? Photographic technology at the time was unable to capture movement, but for years many historians claimed this photograph depicts Federal artillery (guns on the right, with battery horses on the left side of the image) during the Battle of Antietam. Note what was widely believed to be gun smoke hanging in the air. It is now widely believed that this was taken on the day after the fighting ended.

(Bottom) This peaceful scene next to Burnside's Bridge along Antietam Creek belies the horrors that occurred there on September 17, 1862. Antietam was the war's single bloodiest day, during which some 23,000 men were killed, wounded, or captured.

Dead Confederate gunners litter the ground following the Battle of Sharpsburg (Antietam). Behind them is the white Dunker Church, which was heavily damaged by artillery and small arms fire. After the battle, the church was used as a hospital.

An artist's rendition of the fighting at Fredericksburg shows Confederates firing from behind the protection of a stone wall on Marye's Heights. Despite several heavy attacks, not a single Union soldier reached the Southern line.

(Top) Confederate soldiers destroyed this railroad bridge over the Rappahannock River at Fredericksburg, Virginia, to thwart any Union advance. When Union General Burnside moved on the city at the end of 1862, his men were forced to build their own bridges—under fire—in order to cross. (Bottom) General Lee put his men and artillery in strong defensive positions, including Marye's Heights, high ground above Fredericksburg. On December 13, 1862, Burnside attacked but was unable to break through. Casualties were more than 12,000 Federals and 5,000 Confederates.

(Top) These two hills, Round Top (background) and Little Round Top, anchored the southern end of the Union defensive line at Gettysburg. On the battle's second day, Union troops rushed to occupy this rocky slope in the face of attacking Confederates, who threatened to turn the Federal left flank. The Union men held on, but only after heavy fighting. (Bottom) Confederate soldiers killed on July 2, 1863, near Little Round Top at a place described as "The Slaughter Pen." These men, likely Georgians or Alabamians, were killed during the unsuccessful attack against the Union left flank.

(Top) Gettysburg's Evergreen Cemetery, with its arched gatehouse, on East Cemetery Hill, a vital sector of the Union line. On the battle's second day, Confederates launched a twilight attack against this area that captured the heights but was eventually beaten back. Four months later, President Lincoln delivered his famous Gettysburg Address here to dedicate the new Soldiers' National Cemetery. (Bottom) As Lee and Meade battled in Pennsylvania, Grant tightened his stranglehold on Vicksburg, Mississippi. Both sides dug in for a siege. This photo shows the dug-outs and cave-like dwellings where soldiers under Union General John Logan bivouacked. The city fell to Grant on July 4, 1863.

(Left) In November 1863, Union soldiers under General U. S. Grant dislodged Braxton Bragg's Confederates from their positions on Lookout Mountain (shown here and often called "The Battle Above the Clouds") and Missionary Ridge.

(Bottom) Lee and Gordon's Mill on the Chickamauga battlefield in North Georgia, where on September 19-20, 1863, Bragg's hard-luck Army of Tennessee scored its only clear-cut victory of the war in the Western Theater.

(Top) Confederates from General Richard Ewell's Corps, Army of Northern Virginia, killed during the horrific fighting of the Spotsylvania Campaign. (Bottom) Two Union soldiers pose for the camera near a "bombproof" shelter outside Petersburg. This fortification was but one of thousands that dotted the miles of defensive works that eventually ringed Richmond and Petersburg during a nine-month siege.

(Top) A young Confederate in the trenches at Petersburg. He was killed during the final assault on the Petersburg lines on April 2, 1865. (Bottom) Looking for a decisive victory early in the campaign, former coal miners in the 48th Pennsylvania tunneled beneath Confederate lines, packed 8,000 pounds of black powder inside, and exploded it. The mine created a crater roughly 170 feet long, 70 feet wide, and 30 feet deep. The Union attackers were trapped inside the smoking hole and slaughtered.

(Top) A Confederate artillerist (foreground) killed in Fort Mahone outside Petersburg, Virginia, on April 1-2, 1865. Note the head of a ramrod on the bottom right. Above him is a young black man also killed during the fighting. His status—whether slave, servant, or civilian—is unknown. (Bottom) In the late fall of 1864, the Confederate Army of Tennessee under General John Bell Hood invaded Tennessee. His ill-conceived effort ended in disaster at Nashville. Here, a mix of soldiers and civilians observe, from a safe distance, the December 1864 battle for Nashville. The fight resulted in a decisive Union victory.

Technology and the War

(Left) Inventor Thaddeus Lowe accepted the position of chief aeronaut of the new U.S. Balloon Corps in 1861. He and his team made some 3,000 flights during the war's first two years, observing and reporting on enemy positions and strengths. Lowe is shown here at Fair Oaks, VA, in the "Intrepid."

(Bottom) The Civil War witnessed the creation of the first organized signal corps, whose members used towers such as this one at Point of Rocks, VA, to communicate over long distances via semaphore flags.

(Top) The telegraph was an effective means of communication. This field station includes operators and orderlies. These men repaired existing lines and created new ones. By June 1865, the Union army had strung more than 6,000 miles of new wire. (Bottom) Newspapers dispatched artists to capture the scenes of camp and combat. Here, Alfred R. Waud of *Harper's Weekly* is shown sketching on the Gettysburg battlefield.

(Top) The impressive Chain Bridge spanned the Potomac River to connect Virginia and Washington D.C. Union artillery batteries guarded the vital structure's approaches throughout the war. (Bottom) This military pontoon bridge across the Appomattox River was one of many such structures built during the war. On the campaign, armies traveled with a supply of pontoon boats, ready to deploy them whenever a wide river required crossing.

(Top) Railroads were a key means of transporting supplies and manpower during the war. To slow enemy movements, armies on both sides targeted railroad track for destruction. This image shows a repair crew hard at work outside Murfreesboro, Tennessee, not far from the Stones River battlefield. (Bottom) Union soldiers guard a train packed with military supplies near Manassas, Virginia.

When railroads were not an option, the armies relied on horse-drawn wagons to move supplies. This historic image shows the first Union supply train to enter Petersburg, Virginia, after the city's fall on April 2, 1865.

Weapons of War

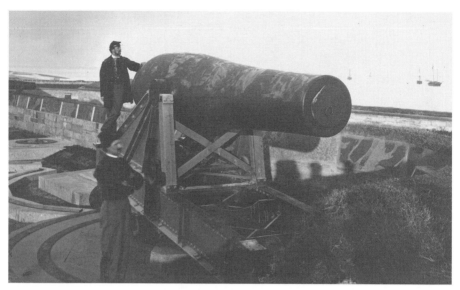

(Top) Before the war, Army officer Thomas Rodman invented a process to manufacture extremely large iron cannon. In 1861, the first 15-inch gun, shown here, was completed under Rodman's supervision and mounted at Fort Monroe, Virginia. (Bottom) The business end of a Confederate cannon, shown in an embrasure in the defenses of Atlanta, Georgia. As the war dragged on, the armies increasingly relied on elaborate fortifications, which provided a measure of protection to their men—and their heavy weapons.

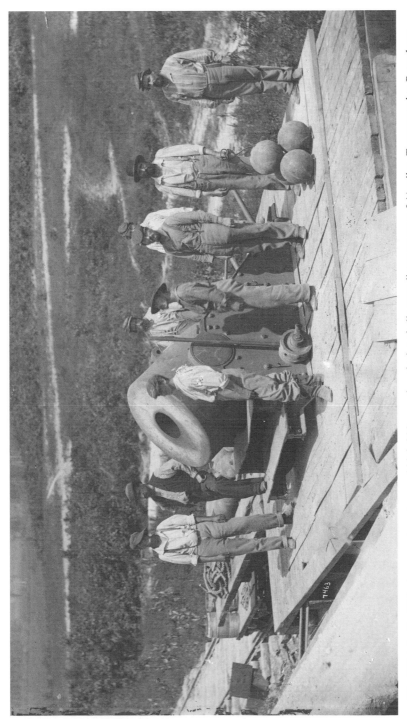

The "Dictator," a 13-inch seacoast mortar, could lob 200-pound explosive shells over distances up to 2 ½ miles. Transported to Petersburg on a reinforced railcar, the "Dictator" fired 19 rounds during the Battle of the Crater.

(Top) Soldiers of 4th New York Heavy Artillery pose beside their 24-pounder siege gun. The projectile of a 24-pounder cannon weighed 24 pounds.

(Center) When fired from a cannon, grapeshot (like canister) offered a shotgun-like effect, sending a shower of small iron balls against enemy soldiers.

(Left) In 1861, William Ketchum designed hand grenades for use by Union troops. The so-called Ketchum Grenades came in one-, three-, and five-pound sizes. Upon impact with a solid surface, a percussion cap in the plunger (nose) detonated the black powder charge in the body. These (and other style) grenades saw use at Vicksburg and Petersburg.

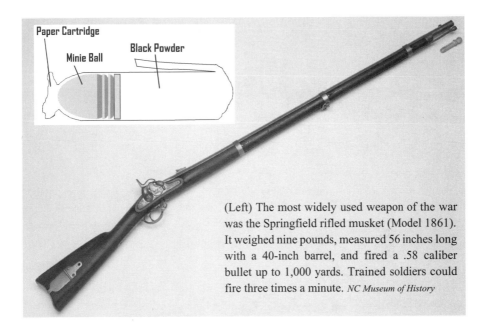

(Left) The most widely used weapon of the war was the Springfield rifled musket (Model 1861). It weighed nine pounds, measured 56 inches long with a 40-inch barrel, and fired a .58 caliber bullet up to 1,000 yards. Trained soldiers could fire three times a minute. *NC Museum of History*

(Insets) Both the Springfield and Enfield fired a lead projectile known as a "minie ball," named after its inventor, French army Captain Claude-Etienne Minié. Soldiers carried minie balls in a paper or linen cartridge that contained a black powder charge. To load a rifled musket, the soldier tore the powder end of the cartridge, poured it down the barrel, inserted the ball (pointed end up), and rammed it down the barrel. Upon firing, the hollow base of the bullet expanded and gripped the barrel's rifling, causing it to spin as it exited the weapon. The spin resulted in increased range and accuracy.

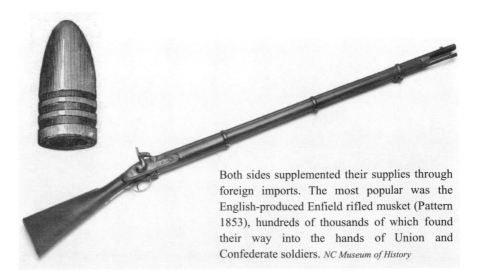

Both sides supplemented their supplies through foreign imports. The most popular was the English-produced Enfield rifled musket (Pattern 1853), hundreds of thousands of which found their way into the hands of Union and Confederate soldiers. *NC Museum of History*

The .52 caliber breech-loading Sharps (an 1859 model is pictured here) was considered the most accurate rifle of the war. The men of the 1st and 2nd U.S. Sharpshooters carried the Sharps, which could fire 8 to 10 rounds per minute. *United States Army, Rock Island Arsenal Museum, Rock Island, Illinois*

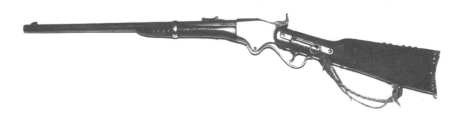

Another rapid-fire weapon was the Spencer Repeating Carbine, which utilized a tubular magazine in its stock that held seven cartridges. A lever ejected the spent round and loaded a new one into the chamber. By war's end, the U.S. Quartermaster's Corps had purchased more than 75,000 Spencers and 60 million cartridges. *United States Army, Rock Island Arsenal Museum, Rock Island, Illinois*

(Left, top) Arguably the most common sidearm of the Civil War, the .36 caliber Colt 1851 "Navy" Revolver, a six-shot, muzzle-loading pistol, was used by soldiers and sailors on both sides.   (Left, bottom) Also popular was Colt's .44 caliber 1860 "Army" Revolver. *United States Army, Rock Island Arsenal Museum, Rock Island, Illinois*

War on the Water

(Top) One observer described the USS *Monitor* as a "cheese box on a raft." Others referred to it as "Ericsson's Folly," after its designer, Swedish-born engineer John Ericsson. This photo shows the *Monitor*'s crew gathered on deck. The ship's low profile made monitors difficult targets, but left them vulnerable in heavy seas. The *Monitor* sank in stormy weather off the North Carolina coast in December 1862. Ericsson's creation ushered the new age of iron warships—and the beginning of the end for wooden vessels. (Bottom) The USS *Onondaga*, a monitor-class ship, on the James River in 1864.

(Top) When U.S. forces abandoned Virginia's Norfolk Navy Yard in April 1861, they burned the frigate USS *Merrimack* to prevent her from falling into enemy hands. The Confederates, however, raised the vessel, rebuilt her as an ironclad ram, and renamed her the CSS *Virginia*. On March 8, 1862, the *Virginia* attacked the wooden U.S. warships guarding Hampton Roads, sinking the USS *Cumberland* (as depicted here) in the process. The following day, the Union's own ironclad, USS *Monitor*, fought the *Virginia* to a stalemate, an engagement that inaugurated a new era in naval warfare.

(Bottom) The Confederate submarine *H. L. Hunley* was the first to sink a ship in wartime. On February 17, 1864, *Hunley* rammed a torpedo into the side of the USS *Housatonic* off Charleston, South Carolina, sending the blockading Union warship and several of her crew to the bottom. The *Hunley*, however, also sank for reasons that remain unclear. Her location was found in 1995, she was raised in 2000, and is today on display in Charleston.

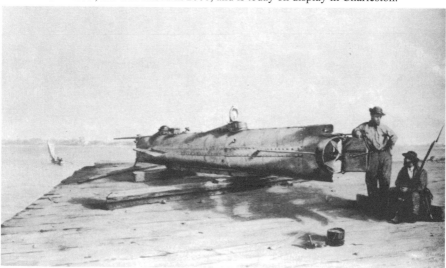

(Top) The crew of the USS *Kearsarge*. In June 1864, she sank the Confederate raider *Alabama* off the coast of France. (Bottom) The CSS *Shenandoah* traveled far and wide during the war, intercepting commerce on the high seas. Here, she is shown in port in Melbourne, Australia. The *Shenandoah* did not surrender until November 1865, nearly seven months after Appomattox. *Photos courtesy of the Naval History & Heritage Collection*

(Top) Boys often served as powder monkeys, carrying gunpowder and shot to gun crews during battle. This lad poses aboard his vessel, the USS *New Hampshire*. (Bottom) USS *Fort Hindman*, a 286-ton side-wheel "tinclad" river gunboat that patrolled western rivers. Without support from gunboats like this, Vicksburg might not have fallen.

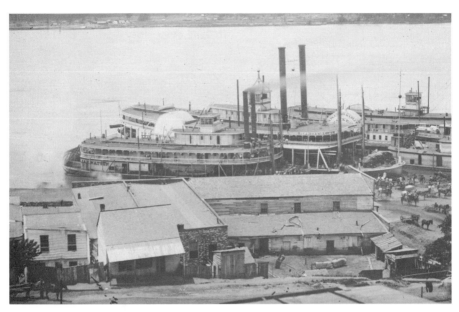

(Top) The July 1863 Union victories at Vicksburg (Mississippi) and Port Hudson (Louisiana) opened the length of the vital Mississippi River to Union shipping, severing the Confederacy in two. Here, a mass of U.S. steamboats rest in port at Vicksburg. Wagons waiting to unload goods can be seen on the right. (Bottom) Amphibious operations during the Civil War were considered the domain of the Army, not the Marine Corps. Though some Marines fought at First Bull Run, for most of the war they served as gun crews on military vessels. Here, Marines pose at the Navy Yard in Washington D.C.

(Top) This is the last known picture of the doomed steamboat *Sultana*. On April 27, 1865, one of the ship's boilers exploded, triggering a raging fire that led to her sinking in the swollen Mississippi River. Some 1,700-1,800 of the ship's 2,000-plus passengers, most of whom were Union soldiers recently released from Confederate prisons, perished. Despite the horrifying losses, the sinking of the *Sultana* remains one of the least publicized disasters of the war. (Bottom) A derelict Confederate *David*-type torpedo boat lies abandoned in Charleston, South Carolina, after Union troops occupied the city in 1865. The 50-foot CSS *David* operated on a steam engine with a crew of four. It was armed with a torpedo extending from her bow on a long wooden spar. In 1863 and 1864, the *David* attacked Union warships blockading Charleston Harbor. Unfortunately, no examples of these torpedo boats exist today.

Caring for the Sick, Wounded, and Dead

(Top) This image shows members of the U.S. Ambulance Corps demonstrating how wounded soldiers were removed from the battlefield. Things rarely went so orderly in battle, during which musicians often served as stretcher-bearers. (Bottom) After treatment in the field, seriously wounded patients were transferred to more substantial facilities, such as the Armory Square Hospital in Washington D.C.

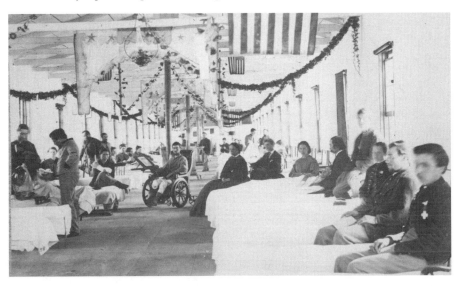

(Top) When General U. S. Grant led the Army of the Potomac into the Wilderness, General Robert E. Lee's Army of Northern Virginia moved to intercept it. What followed was one of the most brutal and bloody battles of the war. These Union soldiers were wounded in the fighting (May 5-6, 1864) and await treatment outside a temporary hospital. (Bottom) Confederates captured many of these convalescing Federal soldiers, who were seized during the Seven Days' fighting on the Virginia peninsula in late June 1862. This image shows a field hospital at Savage's Station, Virginia, which fell to the Southerners after the Union army abandoned the battlefield.

(Top) A woman named Anne Bell helps a pair of wounded Union soldiers in a Nashville, Tennessee, hospital. Many women on both sides of the Mason-Dixon Line volunteered to serve in this capacity. (Bottom) An embalming surgeon named Richard Burr stands over an unidentified soldier's body. Contrary to popular belief, embalming was performed during the Civil War, largely because many families wanted to transport the remains of loved ones long distances for burial at home.

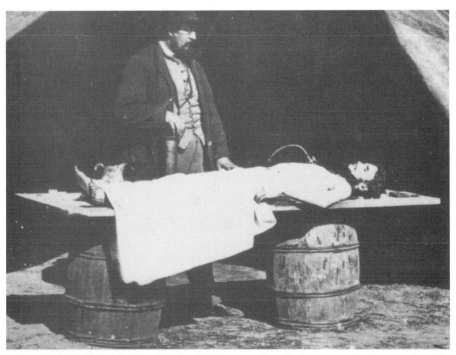

Prisoners of War

(Top) The infamous prison at Andersonville, Georgia. The 26-acre camp housed more than 32,000 Union troops by August 1864. At least 12,920 perished there, as did 115 Confederate guards. While more soldiers died at Andersonville than at any other Civil War prison, Northern prison pens had a higher prisoner mortality rate than their Southern counterparts. During February 1863, nearly 10 percent of Confederate prisoners held at Chicago's Camp Douglas (pictured above) died.

(Top) Early in the war, both sides agreed to a system of prisoner exchange, which helped alleviate crowding in prisons. When the system broke down, authorities on both sides were ill-prepared to deal with the increased numbers of captives. In Elmira, New York, Confederate prisoners were housed in tents while awaiting the construction of proper barracks. Many did not survive the cold winter.

(Left) The 60th Ohio Infantry's John Schumm was one of the 3,504 Union soldiers who died in the pen at Salisbury, North Carolina. In 1873, Congress voted to erect a monument to the 11,700 "unknown" soldiers buried there.

(Top) In one of the most widely recognized photos of the war, these three Confederates, survivors of the carnage at Gettysburg, are about to be transported to a Union POW camp. Malnutrition, disease, and cruel treatment awaited them. Their identity, or whether they survived, is unknown. (Bottom) Richmond's Libby Prison was a converted warehouse used to hold captured Union officers. (Federal authorities exiled Confederate officers to Johnson's Island in Lake Erie.)

Civilians Caught up in the War

(Top) Mrs. Judith Henry, 85, was the first civilian causality of a major battle. An invalid, she remained in her house as the battle of First Bull Run swirled around it. Union artillery destroyed the structure, the remains of which are shown in this March 1862 image. (Below) Former Gettysburg constable John Burns was over 70 when the Confederates invaded his town. During the battle he fought alongside the famous Iron Brigade before being wounded and captured. While in Gettysburg months later, President Lincoln asked to meet the "Old Hero of Gettysburg."

The caption attached to this negative reads "Departure from the old homestead." Note the old woman in the center smoking a pipe, while the woman on the wagon appears to be holding a baby. Tens of thousands of civilians were dislocated during the war. Many did not return.

(Right) When he received word that his soldier-brother had been wounded, poet Walt Whitman rushed to the nation's capital to find him. Touched by the suffering of the soldiers he encountered in the city's overcrowded hospitals, the famous poet volunteered his services as a nurse. By war's end, he claimed to have cared for or visited between 80,000 and 100,000 sick and wounded troops.

(Left) Slaveholder and ardent secessionist Edmund Ruffin was 69 years old when he claimed to have fired the first shot at Fort Sumter. Unwilling to live under "Yankee rule" once the war was lost, he penned several lines in his diary about the war's outcome, wrapped a Confederate flag around his shoulders, and put a bullet into his brain.

(Left) South Carolinian Mary Boykin Chesnut is the most famous diarist of the Civil War. Her keen observations of politics, economics, the course of the war, and especially many of the South's leading personalities makes her book *Mary Chesnut's Civil War* one of the most popular ever published.

(Right) Reverend Dr. William Wilberforce Lord, a native of New York, ended up in Vicksburg, Mississippi, where he served as the minister of the Episcopalian Christ Church and as chaplain in the Confederate army. He and his family endured the terrors of the Vicksburg siege.

The privately funded United States Christian Commission enlisted an army of civilians to help improve the condition of Union soldiers. USCC volunteers provided them with food and reading materials, staffed hospitals, and promoted good health and hygiene. This commission field headquarters was located near Germantown, Virginia.

Women and the War

(Top) Women, most commonly the wives of soldiers, were a common sight in army camps—both as visitors and workers. Here, a woman poses with her soldier-husband and their children.

(Left) Before she founded the American Red Cross, Clara Barton nursed wounded Union soldiers on the battlefield. At Antietam, she arrived with 30 lanterns and hundreds of candles so that mortally wounded soldiers would not die in the dark.

(Left) Mary Emma Hurlbut, her husband General John A. Rawlins, and their daughter at City Point, Virginia, in 1865. Rawlins, a prominent staff officer who closely assisted General U. S. Grant, during most of the war, met Mary in Vicksburg in 1863. Mary, who was born in Danbury, Connecticut, would outlive her husband, who died of tuberculosis in 1869.

(Right) Rose O'Neal Greenhow is best known as a Confederate spy. She was imprisoned for espionage (she is shown here with her daughter in Washington D.C.'s Old Capital Prison in 1862), but earned her freedom and resumed her activities on behalf of the Confederacy. During a mission in 1864, she drowned when the rowboat she boarded while attempting to elude the Federal blockade capsized off the North Carolina coast.

(Top) Not all army nurses were demure. When a Union surgeon questioned her authority, Mary Ann Ball Bickerdyke reportedly replied, "On the authority of Lord God Almighty, have you anything that outranks that?" Called "mother" by grateful men serving with the Western armies, Bickerdyke cared for the wounded on at least nineteen battlefields. (Right) Though she graduated from medical school in 1855, Mary Edwards Walker was allowed only to practice as a nurse during the war's early months. By war's end, she had risen to army surgeon, the first American woman ever to hold the position.

Their men off to war, women were left to run households and raise children alone. Some entered the workforce. Many faced the cruel realities associated with the wounding or death of a loved one. Here, young women gather around Confederate Stonewall Jackson's grave. As losses mounted, similar scenes occurred on both sides. *Virginia Military Institute Archives*

(Left) Some women, like Kady Brownell, were as determined as their husbands to serve in the military. In 1861, after her husband joined the Union army, Kady convinced the governor of Rhode Island to let her accompany him to Washington D.C. His company, part of the 1st Rhode Island Infantry, took Kady on as its color bearer, a position she held at First Bull Run in July 1861. She and her husband continued serving —and saw more action—until his discharge for wounds received in December 1862. *The Louise Arnold Collection, U.S. Army Military Historical Society*

Mary Todd Lincoln (top) and Varina Howell Davis (bottom). Both "First Ladies" lost children during the Civil War. Joseph, the young son of Jefferson and Varina, died after a tragic fall in 1864 at the Confederate White House in Richmond, Virginia. William "Willie" Lincoln, son of Abraham and Mary, died after a brief illness in February 1862.

African Americans and the War

COME AND JOIN US BROTHERS.
PUBLISHED BY THE SUPERVISORY COMMITTEE FOR RECRUITING COLORED REGIMENTS

(Top) Some 180,000 black men served as Union soldiers during the war. Regulations required that the regiments in which they enlisted were commanded by white officers, as illustrated by this call for black recruits. (Bottom) Freed blacks, wearing Union uniform clothing, working for the Army as teamsters.

Two African American soldiers pose in combat positions while on picket duty at Dutch Gap, Virginia, not far from Petersburg and Richmond.

The service of former slaves and free men in uniform did not end with the Civil War. Many volunteered for service and were sent west to battle Indians. The Cheyenne called them "Buffalo soldiers."

(Top) A black cook watches his boiling pots in camp at City Point, Virginia. Many slaves who escaped to Union lines, known as contrabands, found employment with the army. (Bottom) Black families waiting along the east side of the flooded Mississippi River for a ride across to the western bank and, hopefully, a better life in freedom.

Despite the enormous risks involved, many thousands of the nation's four million slaves sought freedom by fleeing to Union lines. Here, former slaves arrive by boat in Union-occupied Richmond, Virginia, in search of a life in freedom.

(Top) Former slaves on the deck of a U.S. warship. Unlike the divisions within the Army, the U.S. Navy had a long history of allowing blacks to serve with white crews. During the war's early months, "contrabands" began enlisting for service aboard military vessels. An estimated 18,000 served in the Union navy during the war. (Bottom) Blacks gathered at Hilton Head, South Carolina, in May 1862.

The Civil War and Native Americans

Cherokee Chief Stand Watie made the rank of brigadier general in the Confederate army. He was one of only two Native Americans to rise to the rank of general (the other was Union General Ely S. Parker). Watie played a prominent role at the Arkansas battle of Pea Ridge on March 6-8, 1862, where his men captured enemy artillery pieces. He participated in the fighting at Cabin Creek in September 1864, the most decisive Confederate victory in Indian Territory. Watie did not surrender until June 23, 1865, the last Confederate general to officially capitulate.

Ely S. Parker was a Seneca Indian, Union general, and U. S. Grant's military secretary. Parker (second from right) penned the document that effectively ended the Civil War when he transcribed the surrender papers signed at Appomattox Court House. Parker was the only Native American Union general.

Both sides utilized Native Americans as scouts and sharpshooters. These Indian sharpshooters, wounded at the Second Battle of Fredericksburg in May 1863, await medical treatment with their white comrades.

(Left) In 1862, Little Crow, leader of the Sioux in Minnesota, was a leading participant in the attempt to drive whites from the state. The four-month conflict, popularly known as the Dakota War, cost the lives of hundreds of civilians, soldiers, and Sioux.

A delegation of Southern Plains Indians during a visit to the White House in March 1863. Seated in the front row (left to right): War Bonnet, Standing in the Water, Lean Bear (all Southern Cheyenne), and Yellow Wolf (Kiowa). Within 18 months, all four would be dead: pneumonia took Yellow Wolf, soldiers killed Lean Bear after mistaking him for a hostile Indian, and War Bonnet and Standing in the Water died during the Sand Creek Massacre in Colorado.

The War Ends

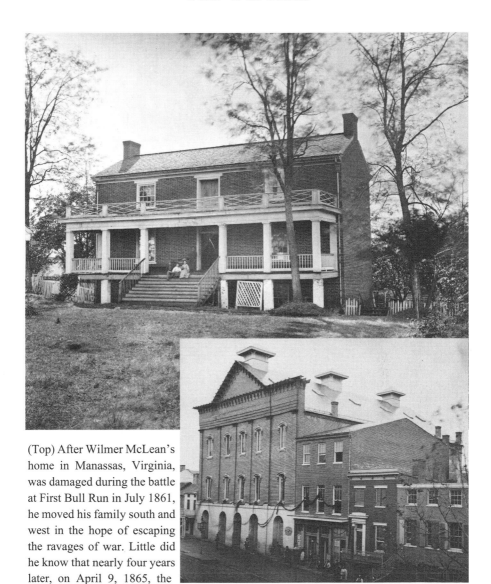

(Top) After Wilmer McLean's home in Manassas, Virginia, was damaged during the battle at First Bull Run in July 1861, he moved his family south and west in the hope of escaping the ravages of war. Little did he know that nearly four years later, on April 9, 1865, the long and bloody conflict would swirl around his property and finally end inside his front parlor when General Robert E. Lee surrendered his Army of Northern Virginia to General U.S. Grant at Appomattox Court House. (Bottom) Northern jubilation was short-lived. Five days after Lee's surrender, actor and Confederate sympathizer John Wilkes Booth shot President Lincoln at Ford's Theater (exterior view above), where he was attending a play with his wife.

(Top) Mortally wounded by a pistol shot to the head, President Lincoln was carried from the Presidential Box at Ford's Theater (shown here) to a boarding house across the street, where he died the next morning.

(Right) Assassin John Wilkes Booth. After shooting the president, Booth jumped to the stage, cried out "Sic semper tyrannis" (Latin for "Thus always to tyrants") and escaped the building. He was later trapped and killed in a barn in Northern Virginia. His primary co-conspirators were tried and executed.

Reconstruction

The immediate postwar period (1865-1877) soon became known as Reconstruction, during which the U.S. government grappled with issues surrounding reconciliation and race in the former states of the Southern Confederacy. Southerners derogatorily called the Northern whites who flocked to the region looking for opportunities (mainly financial) during this period "Carpetbaggers," after the bags in which many of them carried their belongings. One such man was Joseph Rodman West (right). A longtime Philadelphia resident and former Union general, West returned to his native New Orleans after the war and was elected to the U.S. Senate on the Republican ticket.

Southerners who aided Carpetbaggers during Reconstruction were referred to as Scalawags. South Carolinian Alexander Stuart Wallace (left) remained a staunch Unionist during the war. Once it ended, he was elected to the U.S. House of Representatives as a Republican. Wallace served four terms before being defeated in 1876. Wallace's son, George, served as a captain in the U.S. 7th Cavalry during the Indian Wars. He was killed at the Battle of Wounded Knee on December 29, 1890.

The son of slaves, Joseph Rainey (left) worked as a barber in South Carolina before the war. To avoid being impressed into service as a laborer by the Confederate government, Rainey escaped with his wife to the West Indies in 1862. After the conflict, the couple returned to South Carolina. In 1870, Rainey became the first black man ever to be elected to the U.S. House of Representatives. The gains for blacks in the post-Civil War South would prove tenuous, however. By 1900, Southern "redeemers" had all but wiped away the civil and political rights won by blacks shortly after the war.

In 1865, the American Missionary Association established the Fisk School in Nashville, Tennessee, to educate former slaves. Two years later it was chartered as Fisk University. Strapped for cash in 1871, the university sent its Jubilee Singers on a fundraising trip, the proceeds of which were put toward the raising of Jubilee Hall, the first permanent building constructed for educating African Americans in the South.

SECTION III: FIGURES

Numbers and Losses

	UNION	CONFEDERACY[1]
Population	22,400,000	9,103,000[2]
Population of Military Age (18-45)	4,600,000	985,000
Total Number of Enlistments	2,778,326[3]	1,300,000
Army	2,677,119	1,000,000
Navy	101,207	3,000
Marines	3,000	600
Total Deaths	359,528	219,000
Killed in Battle	67,088	53,000
Mortally Wounded	43,012	37,000
Died of Disease	224,586	120,000
Killed in Accidents	4,114	3,000
Drowned	4,944	3,500
Died of Other Known Causes[4]	3,663	2,500
Died of Unknown Causes	12,121	...
Died as Prisoner of War[5]	25,971	27,000
Wounded (not mortally)	275,000	226,000
Captured	211,400	462,000
Deserted[6]	199,000	104,000
Discharged[7]	426,500	57,800
Surrendered in 1865		174,223

1. Estimate based on the most complete data available.

2. Includes 3,760,000 slaves in the states that seceded from the Union.

3. Does not account for Union soldiers who re-enlisted after original terms of service (from three months to three years) expired. Confederates enlisted for the duration of the war.

4. Includes (but is not limited to) murder, suicide, sunstroke, and execution.

5. Represents the number of total deaths for both sides pertaining to prisoners of war.

6. Many Union soldiers enlisted to receive a cash bounty. "Bounty Jumpers" deserted after being paid and repeated the process with another unit.

7. Soldiers discharged for reasons other than the expiration of their terms of service.

Strength of the Union Army

The total strength of the armies on both sides fluctuated during the war. Below are figures on U.S. Army strength—both Regulars and volunteers—taken at various points throughout the war.

DATE	REGULAR ARMY	VOLUNTEERS	TOTAL
Jan. 1, 1861	16,367	0	16,367
July 1, 1861	16,422	170,329	186,751
Jan. 1, 1862	22,425	553,492	575,917
March 31, 1862	23,308	613,818	637,126
Jan. 1, 1863	25,463	892,728	918,191
Jan. 1, 1864	24,636	836,101	860,737
Jan. 1, 1865	22,019	937,411	959,430
March 31, 1865	21,669	958,417	980,086
May 1, 1865	...	...	1,000,516

Unfortunately, no accurate data for the Confederate army exists because of poor record-keeping and lost or destroyed accountings. Depending upon the source, estimates of how many men served in gray at any time during the war range from as low as 500,000 to as high as 2,000,000. The earliest report from the Confederate War Department is at the end of 1861 (326,768 men under arms), followed by 1862 (449,439), 1863 (464,646), 1864 (400,787), and "last reports" (358,692). The best estimates of enlistments throughout the war are 1,227,890 to 1,406,180. (Eicher and Eicher, *Civil War High Commands*, p. 71)

Losses in Major Battles

The charts that begin on the facing page detail the dates, battles, and killed, wounded, captured/missing for both armies in all the major battles of the war.

DATE	BATTLE	UNION ARMY				CONFEDERATE ARMY			
		Killed	Wounded	Missing/Captured	Total	Killed	Wounded	Missing/Captured	Total
1861									
July 21	Bull Run, Va	481	1,011	1,460	2,952	387	1,582	12	1,981
Aug. 10	Wilson's Creek, Missouri	223	721	294	1,238	257	900	27	1,184
Sept. 12 - 20	Lexington, Missouri	42	108	1,624	1,774	…	…	…	100
Oct. 21	Ball's Bluff, Va	223	226	445	894	…	…	…	202
Nov. 7	Belmont, Missouri	90	173	235	498	…	…	…	966
1862									
Feb. 14 - 16	Fort Donelson, TN	446	1,735	150	2,331	2,000 total		14,623	16,623
March 6 - 8	Pea Ridge, AR.	203	972	174	1,349	…	…	…	5,240
March 14	Newbern, NC	91	466	…	557	…	…	…	583
March 23	Winchester, Va	103	440	24	567	…	…	…	691
April 6 - 7	Shiloh, Tn.	1,735	7,882	3,956	13,573	1,723	8,012	959	10,694
May 5	Williamsburg, Va.	456	1,400	372	2,228	1,570 total		133	1,703
May 23	Front Royal, Va.	32	122	800	954	…	…	…	56
May 25	Winchester, Va.	38	155	1,900	2,093	…	…	…	400
May 31 - June 1	Seven Pines / Fair Oaks, Va.	890	3,627	1,222	5,739	980	4,749	405	6,134

DATE	BATTLE	UNION ARMY				CONFEDERATE ARMY			
		Killed	Wounded	Missing/Captured	Total	Killed	Wounded	Missing/Captured	Total
1862									
June 8	Cross Keys, Va.	125	500	...	625	...	...	...	287
June 9	Port Republic, Va.	67	361	574	1,002	...	...	...	657
June 16	Secessionville (James Island), SC	85	472	128	685	...	...	...	204
June 27	Oak Grove, Va.	51	401	64	516	...	...	...	541
June 26 - July 1	Seven Days' Battles	1,582	7,709	5,958	15,249	3,478	16,261	875	20,614
July 13	Murfreesboro, Ten.	33	62	800	895	...	...	...	150
Aug. 8	Cedar Mountain, Va.	450	660	290	1,400	231	1,107	...	1,338
July 26 - Sept. 20	Guerilla campaign in Missouri; includes skirmishes with Porter's and Poindexter's guerillas	77	156	347	580	...	...	...	2,866
Aug. 30 & Sept. 1	2nd Bull Run & Chantilly, Va.	1,724	8,372	5,958	16,054	1,481	7,627	89	9,197
Aug. 30	Richmond, Ky.	200	700	4,000	4,900	78	372	1	451
Sept. 12 - 15	Harpers Ferry, Va.	80	120	11,583	11,783	...	...	...	500

DATE	BATTLE	UNION ARMY				CONFEDERATE ARMY			
		Killed	Wounded	Missing/Captured	Total	Killed	Wounded	Missing/Captured	Total
1862 continued									
Sept. 14	South Mountain	443	1,806	76	2,325	325	1,560	800	2,685
Sept. 14 - 16	Mumfordsville, Ky.	50	...	3,566	3,616	...	...	...	714
Sept. 17	Antietam, Md.	2,010	9,416	1,043	12,469	2,700	9,024	1,800	13,524
Sept. 17	Iuka, Miss.	144	598	40	782	...	...	...	1,516
Oct. 3 - 4	Corinth, Miss.	315	1,812	232	2,359	473	1,997	1,763	4,233
Oct. 5	Big Hatchie River, Miss.	...	...	...	500	...			400
Oct. 8	Perryville, Ky.	916	2,943	489	4,348	510	2,635	251	3,396
Dec. 7	Prairie Grove, Ark.	167	798	183	1,148	164	817	336	1,317
Dec. 7	Hartsville, Ten.	55	...	1,800	1,855	...	...	...	149
Dec. 12 - 18	Foster's expedition to Goldsboro, NC	90	478	9	577	...	...	...	739
Dec. 13	Fredericksburg, Va.	1,180	9,028	2,145	12,353	595	4,061	653	5,309
Dec. 20	Holly Springs, Miss.	...	...	1,000	1,000	...	...	...	...
Dec. 27	Elizabethtown, Ky.	...	...	...	500	...	...	...	...

DATE	BATTLE	UNION ARMY				CONFEDERATE ARMY			
		Killed	Wounded	Missing/ Captured	Total	Killed	Wounded	Missing/ Captured	Total
1862 continued									
Dec. 28 - 29	Chickasaw Bayou, Miss.	191	982	756	1,929	63	134	10	207
Dec. 31 - Jan. 2, 1863	Stones River, Ten.	1,533	7,245	2,800	11,578	1,294	7,945	2,476	11,715
1863									
Jan. 1	Galveston, Tex.	...	...	600	600	...	...	...	50
Jan. 11	Fort Hindman - Arkansas Post, Ark.	129	831	17	977	28	81	4,791	4,900
Jan. 4 - 5	Thompson's Station, Ten.	100	300	1,306	1,706				600
April 27 - May 3	Streight's raid from Tuscumbia, Ala., to Rome, Ga.	12	69	1,466	1,547	...	...	...	...
May 1 - 4	Port Gibson, Miss.	130	718	5	853	...	...	...	1,650
May 1 - 4	Chancellorsville, Va.	1,512	9,518	5,000	16,030	1,665	9,081	2,018	12,764
May 14	Jackson, Miss.	100	800	100	1,000	...	...	...	1,359
May 16	Champion Hill, Miss.	426	1,842	189	2,457	381	1,769	1,670	3,820

DATE	BATTLE	UNION ARMY				CONFEDERATE ARMY			
		Killed	Wounded	Missing/Captured	Total	Killed	Wounded	Missing/Captured	Total
1863 continued									
May 18 - July 4	Siege of Vicksburg, Miss.	545	3,688	303	4,536	...	...	...	31,277
May 27 - July 9	Siege of Port Hudson, La.	500	2,500	...	3,000	...	...	...	7,208
June 6 - 8	Milliken's Bend, La.	154	223	115	492	...	...	...	725
June 9	Brandy Station and Beverly Ford, Va.	...	...	...	500	...	...	...	700
June 13 - 15	Winchester, Va.	...	...	3,000	3,000	...	...	...	850
June 14	Federal attack at Port Hudson including the siege of Port Hudson (above)	203	1,401	188	1,792	22	25	...	47
June 23 - 30	Rosecrans' campaign from Murfreesboro to Tullahoma, Ten.	85	462	13	560	...	...	...	1,634
July 1 - 3	Gettysburg, Pen.	2,834	13,709	6,643	23,186	3,903	18,735	5,425	28,063
July 18	Fort Wagner, SC	...	...	...	1,500	36	133	5	174
Sept. 19 - 20	Chickamauga, Ga.	1,644	9,262	4,945	15,851	2,312	14,674	1,468	18,454

DATE	BATTLE	UNION ARMY				CONFEDERATE ARMY			
		Killed	Wounded	Missing/Captured	Total	Killed	Wounded	Missing/Captured	Total
1863 continued									
Nov. 3	Grand Coteau, La.	26	124	576	726	...	...	...	445
Nov. 6	Rogersville, Ten.	5	12	650	667	...	...	...	30
Nov. 23 - 25	Chattanooga, Ten. - (Orchard Knob, Lookout Mountain, Missionary Ridge)	757	4,529	320	5,606	361	2,160	4,146	6,667
Nov. 26 - 28	Mine Run, Va.	173	1,099	381	1,653	110	570	65	745
Dec. 14	Bean's Station, Va.	...	...	700	700	...	...	...	900
1864									
Feb. 20	Olustee, Fla.	193	1,175	460	1,828	93	841	...	934
April 8	Sabine Cross Roads, La.	200	900	1,800	2,900	...	...	...	1,500
April 9	Pleasant Hills, La.	150	844	375	1,369	About 1,000 total		500	1,500
April 12	Fort Pillow, Ten.	350	60	164	574	...	...	...	80
April 17 - 20	Plymouth, NC	20	80	1,500	1,600	...	...	...	500
April 30	Jenkins' Ferry, Ark.	200	955	...	1,155	...	...	...	1,100

DATE	BATTLE	UNION ARMY				CONFEDERATE ARMY			
		Killed	Wounded	Missing/Captured	Total	Killed	Wounded	Missing/Captured	Total
1864 continued									
May 5 - 7	Wilderness, Va.	5,597	21,463	10,677	37,737	...	...	...	11,700
May 5 - 9	Northeastern Georgia (Rocky Face Bridge, Tunnel Hill, Mill Creek Gap, Buzzard Roost, Snake Creek, and Dalton actions)	200	637	...	837	...	...	...	600
May 8 - 18	Spotsylvania	4,177	19,687	2,577	26,441	...	...	...	9,000
May 9 - 10	Swift Creek, Va.	90	400	...	490	...	...	...	500
May 9 - 10	Cloyd's Mountain & New River Bridge, Va.	126	585	34	745	...	...	...	900
May 12 - 16	Fort Darling (Drury's Bluff), Va.	422	2,380	210	3,012	...	...	...	2,560
May 13 - 16	Resaca, Ga.	600	2,147	...	2,747	...	...	...	2,800
May 15	New Market, Va.	120	560	240	920	...	...	...	405
May 16 - 30	Bermuda Hundred, Va.	200	1,000	...	1,200	...	...	...	3,000

DATE	BATTLE	UNION ARMY				CONFEDERATE ARMY			
		Killed	Wounded	Missing/Captured	Total	Killed	Wounded	Missing/Captured	Total
1864 continued									
May 23 - 27	North Anna River, Va.	223	1,460	290	1,973	...	...	...	2,000
May 25 - June 4	Dallas, Ga.	...	...	2,400	2,400	...	...	...	2,000
June 1 - 12	Cold Harbor, Va.	1,905	10,570	2,456	14,931	...	...	...	1,700
June 5	Piedmont, Va.	130	650	...	780	...	...	...	2,970
June 9 - 30	Kennesaw Mountain, Ga.	1,370	6,500	800	8,670	...	...	...	4,600
June 10	Brices Cross Roads, Miss.	223	394	1,623	2,240	...	...	...	606
June 10	Kellar's Bridge - Licking River, Ky.	13	54	700	767	...	...	...	...
June 11 - 12	Trevilian Station, Va.	85	490	160	735	...	...	...	370
June 15 - 19	Petersburg, Va.	1,298	7,474	1,814	10,586	...	...	...	...
June 17 - 18	Lynchburg, Va.	100	500	400	1,000	...	...	...	200
June 20 - 30	Trenches of Petersburg, Va.	112	506	800	1,418	...	...	...	...

DATE	BATTLE	UNION ARMY				CONFEDERATE ARMY			
		Killed	Wounded	Missing/Captured	Total	Killed	Wounded	Missing/Captured	Total
1864 continued									
June 22 - 30	Wilson's raid on the Weldon Railroad, Va.	76	265	700	1,041	...	...	...	300
June 22 - 23	Weldon Railroad, Va.	604	2,494	2,217	5,315	...	...	...	500
June 27	Kennesaw Mountain, Ga.	...	...	...	3,000	270 total		172	442
July 1 - 31	Petersburg, Va. (Crater and Deep Bottom not included.)	419	2,076	1,200	3,695	...	...	...	...
July 6 - 10	Chattahoochee River, Ga.	80	450	200	730	...	...	...	600
July 9	Monocacy, Md.	90	579	1,290	1,959	...	...	...	400
July 13 - 15	Tupelo, Miss.	85	563	...	648	210	1,116	...	1,326
July 20	Peach Tree Creek, Ga.	300	1,410	...	1,710	...	...	...	4,796
July 22	Atlanta, Ga. - Hood's First Sortie	500	2,141	1,000	3,641	2,890 total		851	3,741
July 24	Winchester, Va.	...	...	...	1,200	...	...	...	600
July 26 - 31	Stoneman's raid to Macon, Ga.	...	100	900	1,000	...	...	...	...

DATE	BATTLE	UNION ARMY				CONFEDERATE ARMY			
		Killed	Wounded	Missing/Captured	Total	Killed	Wounded	Missing/Captured	Total
1864 continued									
July 26 - 31	McCook's raid to Lovejoy's Station, Ga.	...	100	500	600	...	...	...	...
July 28	Ezra Church, Ga. - Hood's Second Sortie	100	600	...	700	...	...	...	4,642
July 30	Mine explosion at Petersburg, Va.	419	1,679	1,910	4,008	...	...	...	1,200
Aug. 1 - 31	Trenches in front of Petersburg, Va.	87	484	...	571	...	...	...	...
Aug. 14 - 13	Strawberry Plains - Deep Bottom Run, Va.	400	1,755	1,400	3,555	...	...	...	1,100
Aug. 18 - 21	Weldon Railroad, Va.	212	1,155	3,176	4,543	...	...	...	1,000
Aug. 21	Forrest's Memphis, Ten.	...	...	550	550	...	...	...	...
Aug. 21	Summit Point, Va.	...	...	...	600	...	...	...	400
Aug. 25	Ream's Station, Va.	127	546	1,769	2,442	...	...	...	720
Aug. 31 - Sept. 1	Jonesboro, Ga.	...	1,149	...	1,419	1,640 total		360	2,000
May 5 - Sept. 8	Sherman's Campaign	5,284	26,129	5,786	37,199	...	...	...	...

DATE	BATTLE	UNION ARMY				CONFEDERATE ARMY			
		Killed	Wounded	Missing/Captured	Total	Killed	Wounded	Missing/Captured	Total
1864 continued									
Sept. 1 - Oct. 31	Trenches in front of Petersburg, Va.	170	822	812	1,804	...	...	...	1,000
Sept. 19	Winchester, Va.	653	3,719	618	4,990	276	1,827	1,818	3,921
Sept. 23	Athens, Ala.	...	...	950	950	...	...	...	30
Sept. 21 - Oct. 28	Price's Missouri Raid	170	336	...	506	...	...	...	...
Sept. 28 - 30	New Market Heights, Va.	400	2,029	...	2,429	...	...	...	2,000
Sept. 30 - Oct. 1	Preble's Farm - Poplar Springs Church, Va.	141	788	1,756	2,685	...	...	...	900
Oct. 5	Allatoona, Ga.	142	352	212	706	320	1,540	1,050	2,910
Oct. 19	Cedar Creek, Va.	588	3,516	1,891	5,995	320	1,540	1,050	2,910
Oct. 27	Hatcher's Run - Southside Railroad, Va.	156	1,047	699	1,902	...	...	...	1,000
Oct. 27 & 28	Fair Oaks - near Richmond, Va.	120	783	400	1,303	...	...	...	451
Nov. 28	New Creek, W. Va.	...	...	700	700	...	...	...	5

DATE	BATTLE	UNION ARMY				CONFEDERATE ARMY			
		Killed	Wounded	Missing/Captured	Total	Killed	Wounded	Missing/Captured	Total
1864 continued									
Nov. 30	Franklin, Ten.	189	1,033	1,104	2,326	1,750	3,800	702	6,252
Nov. 30	Honey Hill, SC	66	645	...	711	...	...	...	...
Dec. 6 - 9	Deveaux's Neck, SC	39	390	200	629	...	...	...	400
Dec. 15 - 16	Nashville, Ten.	400	1,740	...	2,140	1,500 total		4,462	5,962
1865									
Jan. 11	Beverly, W. Va.	5	20	583	608	...	...	...	...
Jan. 13 - 15	Fort Fisher, NC	184	749	22	955	...	...	...	2,483
Feb. 5 - 7	Dabney's Mills - Hatcher's Run, Va.	232	1,062	186	1,480	...	...	...	1,290
March 8 - 10	Wise's Fork, NC	89	421	600	1,110	...	...	...	1,500
March 16	Averasboro, NC	77	477	...	554	...	...	...	865
March 19 - 21	Bentonville, NC	191	1,168	287	1,646	195	1,313	610	2,118
March 25	Fort Steadman - Petersburg, Va.	68	337	506	911	...	...	...	2,681
March 25	Petersburg, Va.	103	864	209	1,176	...	...	...	834

DATE	BATTLE	UNION ARMY				CONFEDERATE ARMY			
		Killed	Wounded	Missing/Captured	Total	Killed	Wounded	Missing/Captured	Total
1865 continued									
March 26 - April 8	Spanish Fort, Ala.	100	695	...	795	...	...	...	552
March 22 - April 24	Wilson's raid from Chickasaw, Ala., to Macon, Ga.	99	598	28	725	...	...	...	8,020
March 31	Boydton & White Oak Roads, Va.	177	1,134	556	1,867	...	...	...	1,235
April 1	Five Forks, Va.	124	706	54	884	...	...	...	8,500
April 6 - 7	Sayler's Creek, High Bridge, Farmville, Va.	176	1,045	1,000	2,221	...	...	...	7,000 (Sayler's Creek)
April 6	Sayler's Creek, Va.	166	1,014	...	1,180	...	...	...	7,000
April 9	Robert E. Lee surrenders					...	...	26,765	26,765
April 26	Joseph E. Johnston surrenders							29,924	29,924
May 4	Richard Taylor surrenders							10,000	10,000
May 26	Kirby Smith surrenders							20,000	20,000

Number of Engagements Fought in Each State and Territory During the Civil War

State / Territory	1861	1862	1863	1864	1865	Total
Alabama	...	10	12	32	24	78
Arizona Territory	...	1	1	1	1	4
Arkansas	1	42	40	78	6	167
California	...	1	4	1	...	6
Colorado Territory	...	...	...	4	...	4
Dakota Territory	...	2	5	4	...	11
District of Columbia	...	...	...	1	...	1
Florida	3	3	4	17	5	32
Georgia	...	2	8	92	6	108
Idaho Territory	...	...	1	...	...	1
Illinois	...	...	...	1	...	1
Indian Territory	...	2	9	3	3	17
Indiana	...	...	4	...	...	4
Kansas	...	...	2	5	...	7
Kentucky	14	59	30	31	4	138
Louisiana	1	11	54	50	2	118
Maryland	3	9	10	8	...	30
Minnesota	...	5	1	...	...	6
Mississippi	...	42	76	67	1	186

State / Territory	1861	1862	1863	1864	1865	Total
Missouri	65	95	43	41	...	244
Nebraska Territory	...	...	2	...	...	2
Nevada	...	...	...	2	...	2
New Mexico Territory	3	5	7	4	...	19
New York	...	...	1	...	...	1
North Carolina	2	27	18	10	28	85
Ohio	...	...	3	...	...	3
Oregon	...	...	...	3	1	4
Pennsylvania	...	...	8	1	...	9
South Carolina	2	10	17	9	22	60
Tennessee	2	82	124	89	1	298
Texas	1	2	8	1	2	14
Utah Territory	...	...	1	...	...	1
Vermont	...	...	...	1	...	1
Virginia	30	140	116	205	28	519
Washington Territory	...	...	1	...	...	1
West Virginia	29	14	17	19	1	80
Totals	**156**	**564**	**627**	**780**	**135**	**2,262**

Alternate Names of Battles

Many battles were called by different names. Usually, the Union employed the name of nearby creeks or rivers (Antietam), while Confederates used nearby towns or cities (Sharpsburg). Both sides referred to the largest battle of the war, Gettysburg, by the same name. Below are some prominent examples.

Name	Alternate Name	State	Year
Bakers Creek	Champion Hill	MS	1863
Battle of the Osage	Mine Creek	KS	1864
Battle of the Poor House	Ezra Church	GA	1864
Beaver Dam Creek	Mechanicsville	VA	1862
Belle Grove	Cedar Creek	VA	1864
Bowers Hill	1st Winchester	VA	1862
Boonsboro	South Mountain	MD	1862
Chaplin Hills	Perryville	KY	1862
Chickahominy	Gaines' Mill	VA	1862
Elkhorn Tavern	Pea Ridge	AR	1862
Fair Oaks	Seven Pines	VA	1862
Fayetteville	Prairie Grove	AR	1862
Fleetwood Hill	Brandy Station	VA	1863
Fort Darling	Drewry's Bluff	VA	1862
Fort Hindman	Arkansas Post	AR	1863
Green River Bridge	Munfordville	KY	1862
Groveton	2nd Manassas	VA	1862
Harrisburg	Tupelo	MS	1864
Honey Springs	Elk Creek	Indian Territory	1863
Logan's Cross Roads	Mill Springs	KY	1862
Manassas (First)	1st Bull Run	VA	1861
Manassas (Second)	2nd Bull Run	VA	1862

Name	Alternate Name	State	Year
Mansfield	Sabine Cross-Roads	LA	1864
Murfreesboro	Stones River	TN	1862
Nelson's Farm	Glendale	VA	1862
Oak Hills	Wilson Creek	MO	1861
Ocean Pond	Olustee	FL	1864
Opequon Creek	Winchester (3rd battle)	VA	1864
Ox Hill	Chantilly	VA	1862
Pittsburg Landing	Shiloh	TN	1862
Poindexter's Farm	Malvern Hill	VA	1862
Pumpkinvine Creek	Dallas	GA	1864
Sabine Cross-Roads	Mansfield	LA	1864
Sharpsburg	Antietam	MD	1862
Thompson's Hill	Port Gibson	MS	1863
Tishomingo Creek	Brices Cross Roads	TN	1864
White Oak Swamp	Glendale	VA	1862

Troops Furnished by the Various States and Territories to the Union Army

As you might expect, different states and territories supplied varying numbers of white troops and sailors, and black troops, for service in either the Union or Confederate armies.

This table indicates these numbers, as well as the deaths attributed to the men raised to fight for the war.

State / Territory	White Troops	Sailors & Marines	Black Troops	Aggregate	Deaths (all causes)
Alabama	2,578	...	...	2,578	345
Arkansas	8,289	...	...	8,289	1,713
California	15,725	...	...	15,725	573
Colorado Territory	4,903	...	...	4,903	323
Connecticut	51,937	2,163	1,784	55,884	5,354
Dakota Territory	206	...	...	206	6
Delaware	11,236	94	954	12,284	882
District of Columbia	11,912	1,353	3,269	16,534	290
Florida	1,290	...	...	1,290	215
Georgia	...	...	...	...	15
Illinois	255,057	2,224	1,811	259,092	34,834
Indiana	193,748	1,078	1,537	196,363	26,672
Iowa	75,797	5	440	76,242	13,001
Kansas	18,069	...	2,080	20,149	2,630
Kentucky	51,743	314	23,703	75,760	10,774
Louisiana	5,224	...	...	5,224	945
Maine	64,973	5,030	104	70,107	9,398

State / Territory	White Troops	Sailors & Marines	Black Troops	Aggregate	Deaths (all causes)
Maryland	33,995	3,925	8,718	46,638	2,982
Massachusetts	122,781	19,983	3,966	146,730	13,942
Michigan	85,479	498	1,387	87,364	14,753
Minnesota	23,913	3	104	24,020	2,584
Mississippi	545	…	…	545	78
Missouri	100,616	151	8,344	109,111	13,885
Nebraska Territory	3,157	…	…	3,157	239
Nevada	1,080	…	…	1,080	33
New Hampshire	32,930	882	125	33,937	4,882
New Jersey	67,500	8,129	1,185	76,814	5,754
New Mexico Territory	6,561	…	…	6,561	277
New York	409,561	35,164	4,125	448,850	46,534
North Carolina	3,156	…	…	3,156	360
Ohio	304,814	3,274	5,092	313,180	35,475
Oregon	1,810	…	…	1,810	45
Pennsylvania	315,017	14,307	8,612	337,936	33,183
Rhode Island	19,521	1,878	1,837	23,236	1,321
Tennessee	31,092	…	…	31,092	8,777
Texas	1,965	…	…	1,965	141
Vermont	32,549	619	120	33,288	5,224
Virginia	…	…	…	…	42
Washington Territory	964	…	…	964	22
West Virginia	31,739	133	196	32,068	4,017
Wisconsin	91,162	…	165	91,327	12,301
Indian Nation	…	…	…	3,530	1,018

State / Territory	White Troops	Sailors & Marines	Black Troops	Aggregate	Deaths (all causes)
Regular Army	...	...	...	...	5,798
United States Colored Troops	...	...	99,337[1]	99,337	34,847[2]
Veteran Volunteers	...	...	...	...	106
U.S. Volunteers[3]	...	...	...	...	243
Sharpshooters & Engineers	...	...	...	...	552
Veterans Reserve Corps	...	...	...	...	1,672
Generals & Staffs	...	...	...	...	239
Misc. - Bands & etc.	...	...	...	...	232
Totals	2,494,594	101,207	178,995	2,778,326[4]	359,528

Notes:

[1] African American soldiers recruited from the South.

[2] This figure includes the deaths of all black soldiers, and not just those who served in USCT regiments.

[3] Also known as "Galvanized Yankees," these former Confederates were recruited largely from Union prison camps.

[4] The enlistments total include 3,530 soldiers from the Indian Nation.

Causes of Battle Wounds

In 1870, the U.S. Army Surgeon General reported on the causes of 246,712 wounds received in battle by Union soldiers. While the list does not account for every wounded Union soldier, or for tens of thousands of dead who were buried on the field without close inspection, it is nevertheless illuminating.

Cause of Wound	Number of Cases	% of Total
Rifle / Musket	124,921	50.6
Cannon	14,032	5.7
Pistol / Buckshot	3,008	1.2
Sabre	522	0.2
Bayonet	400	0.2
Shot *	103,829	42.1

* Source of missile (rifle, cannon, or pistol) not ascertained.

Major Causes of Death

The U.S. Army Surgeon General's 1870 report also included information on the causes of 195,627 non-battle-related Union soldier deaths (excluding those that occurred in Confederate prison camps). They are, in order of frequency:

Cause of Death	Number of Cases Reported	Number of Deaths
Diarrhoea / Dysentery	1,741,914	43,548
Typhoid Fever	79,412	29,336
Inflammation of Lungs	77,335	19,971
Consumption	14,830	6,497
Smallpox	18,952	7,058
Measles	76,318	5,178
Typho-Malarial Fever	62,578	5,360
Remittent Fever	317,135	4,862
Congestive Intermittent Fever	16,209	4,164
Erysipelas	23,276	247
Inflammation of Brain		1,279
Suicide		310
Homicide		174
Execution		143

Principal Union Prisons

In 1912, the Commissioner for Marking Confederate Graves in the North reported a total of 25,560 Confederate soldiers, sailors, and citizens buried in northern states. An unknown number of Confederate prisoners died while in federal custody in southern states.

Prison (location)	Peak Occupancy	Deaths
Alton (IL)	1,721 - February 1865	1,691
Beaufort (SC)		117
Camp Butler (IL)	2,381 - December 1863	866
Camp Chase (Columbus, OH)	9,045 - February 1865	2,248
Camp Douglas (Chicago, IL)	11,762 - January 1865	4,457
Camp Morton (Indianapolis, IN)	4,906 - August 1864	1,638
Chester (PA)		155
Elmira (NY)	9,480 - September 1864	3,022
Fort Columbus (NYC Harbor, NY)		Note 1
Fort Delaware (Pea Patch Island, DE)	9,174 - July 1864	2,475
Fort Lafayette (NYC Harbor, NY)		Note 1
Fort McHenry (Baltimore, MD)		29
Fort Pickens (FL)		
Fort Warren (Boston Harbor, MA)		13
Fort Wood (NYC Harbor, NY)		Note 1
Johnson's Island (OH)	3,204 - January 1865	246 - note 2
Little Rock (AR)		

Prison (location)	Peak Occupancy	Deaths
Louisville (KY)		283
Madison (WI)		140
McLean Barracks (Cincinnati, OH)		
Memphis (TN)		
Nashville (TN)		
New Orleans (LA)	1,691 - September 1864	
Old Capitol (DC)	1,009 - August 1863	Note 3
Point Lookout (MD)	14,489 - July 1864	3,430
Rock Island (IL)	8,344 - August 1864	1,961
Ship Island (MS)		153
Saint Louis (Jefferson Barracks, MO)		1,259
Wheeling (WV)		3

Notes:

1. Some 515 Confederate POWs are buried in Cypress Hills National Cemetery in Brooklyn, New York.

2 . Most of the Confederates held on Johnson's Island were officers.

3. Approximately 400 Confederate POWs died in Washington D.C. during the war.

Principal Confederate Prisons

Many Confederate prison records—including those concerning prisoner deaths—did not survive the war. The figures below come from the *Roll of Honor* series published by the U.S. Quartermaster General after the end of the conflict. A sizeable (but unknown) number of Union soldiers died en route to prison camps or while awaiting transportation to prisons from battlefields.

Name (location)	Deaths
Americus (GA)	not reported
Andersonville (Camp Sumter, GA)	12,461
Atlanta (GA)	124
Augusta (GA)	79
Blackshear (FL)	not reported
Cahaba (AL)	147
Camp Ford (Tyler, TX)	1
Camp Groce (near Hempstead, TX)	not reported
Camp Lawton (Millen, GA)	685
Camp Oglethorpe (Macon, GA)	236
Charleston (SC)	389
Charlotte (NC)	not reported
Columbia (SC)	33
Danville (VA)	778
Florence (SC)	2,793
Lynchburg (VA)	25
Marietta (GA)	189
Mobile (AL)	77
Montgomery (AL)	198

Name (location)	Deaths
Petersburg (VA)	36
Raleigh (NC)	23
Richmond (VA – Belle Isle, Castle Thunder, Crew's, Grant's Factory, Libby, Pemberton's Scott's, and Smith Factory)	3,450[1]
Salisbury (NC)	3,504[2]
Savannah (GA)	2
Shreveport (LA)	not reported
Tuscaloosa (AL)	not reported

Notes

1. In 1868, the U.S. Quartermaster General reported 3,450 POWs buried in the Richmond National Cemetery. Bodies of an additional 3,000-plus Union soldiers were later relocated to the cemetery from battlefields around Richmond.

2. In 1868, the U.S. Quartermaster General reported 3,501 known and 3 unknown Union soldiers buried at Salisbury. Volume 14 of *Roll of Honor* lists these names. However, the next year the U.S. Inspector of National Cemeteries claimed that Salisbury's burial records "cannot be found," and incorrectly estimated that 11,700 soldiers were interred there. Based on these findings, the federal government erected a monument to the "11,700 unknown" Union soldiers buried at Salisbury in 1873.

SECTION IV: MISCELLANY

African Americans in the Civil War

Few people North or South fully understood the wide-ranging roles that blacks, both slave and free, would play in the Civil War. Fewer still predicted the long-lasting effects that the war would have on race issues that linger even today.

When the war began in 1861, nearly everyone in the North believed the struggle was all about preserving the Union. Abolitionists, however, believed a sectional war, or civil war, was the best and possibly the only opportunity to abolish slavery for all time. When the war finally ended in 1865, the long bloody struggle was being waged for both important goals.

The pivot point that turned the Union war effort in the direction of ending slavery began with President Abraham Lincoln's Emancipation Proclamation, issued on January 1, 1863. Lincoln made the important document public after the strategic victory in Maryland the previous fall at Antietam. The proclamation declared that all slaves held within those states in rebellion were now free, though it did not attempt to abolish bondage within the boarder states, Tennessee, or Union-occupied land in other places across the Confederacy. At the time Lincoln's action was considered folly, but it was really a clever political move to shift the focus of the war while making it nearly impossible for England and France to enter the conflict on behalf of the Confederacy; its citizens would not have supported a military effort to fight against a country trying to free slaves.

Slaves and other free blacks (commonly called "contrabands") took an active role in their own future. Many in bondage escaped, especially when Union armies penetrated into Southern territory. These men (and women and occasionally children) often worked for Union armies.

Nearly 180,000 blacks (about one in ten for every man in a Union uniform) served as soldiers, many in regiments designated United Sates Colored Troops (USCT). Most units were commanded by white officers, and black noncommissioned officers. Thousands more blacks served in the U.S. Navy. Most of the men spent the bulk of their service performing support functions, such as carpenters, cooks, teamsters, guards, and laborers. Black women were not allowed to join the Army, but did serve in many other important roles, including nurses and spies.

Because many believed they would not fight well, black units were not used very often in combat roles. Wherever they did fight, however, they fought very well. Battles included: Milliken's Bend, Louisiana (where many were killed after they surrendered); Port Hudson, Louisiana; The Battle of the Crater in Petersburg, Virginia; and at Nashville, Tennessee. The most famous black fighting regiment was the 54th Massachusetts Infantry, which was led by Colonel Robert Gould Shaw. The 54th led the suicidal charge against Battery Wagner in July 1863 on the outskirts of Charleston, South Carolina, a desperate act of valor forever memorialized in the movie Glory. In what most historians believe was an intentional act, Confederate soldiers killed black Union soldiers who tried to surrender in the 1864 fighting at Fort Pillow, Tennessee. By the time the war ended, sixteen black soldiers had been awarded the coveted Medal of Honor.

Many blacks in the South voluntarily remained with their masters, however, tending the plantations and farms while the white men were fighting to keep them enslaved. Some accompanied their owners to the front as servants, a few shouldered muskets on behalf of the South, and thousands more worked behind the lines as laborers. During the war's final weeks, the Confederacy officially agreed to enlist blacks to fight in exchange for their freedom, but nothing came of the effort before the war drew to a close.

Native Americans in the Civil War

Contrary to what many people believe, the war was not fought just in Virginia, Pennsylvania, and Tennessee. In fact, a sprawling and very bloody war was fought west of the Mississippi River (in what was called the Trans-Mississippi Theater), in Indian Territory (in what is today largely the state of Oklahoma), and the New Mexico Territory. Even Minnesota witnessed a frenzy of killing in 1862. Prominent in much of this fighting were Native Americans. What is even less well known is that another civil war was fought across much of the West between various Indian tribes.

The Union and Confederacy recruited and used Native Americans in different ways and for different reasons. Most served in and near Indian Territory and were used to combat Confederate efforts in that region. About 3,500 ultimately served in the Union Army between 1861 and 1865. Units included the 1st through 4th Regiment Indian Home Guard (although organization got underway for the 4th, the unit was never fully completed). Most of these men served on a variety of expeditions and to reinforce forts and far flung outposts. Each was mustered out in May 1865.

The most prominent Union Indian was a member of the Seneca tribe named Ely Parker. An aide to General Ulysses S. Grant, Parker was promoted to general (one of two Indians who held that rank, the other being a Cherokee named Stand Watie who fought for the Confederacy) and was an eyewitness to Robert E. Lee's surrender at Appomattox Court House on April 9, 1865. Parker never held a combat command.

It is more difficult to calculate numbers for Confederate service because records are incomplete and record-keeping in this region was not carefully maintained. The South made alliances with tribes in Indian Territory to raise regiments for service, and to act as a buffer zone for other white troops serving in other states. Chief Stand Watie organized the 1st Cherokee Mounted Rifles and led his regiment in several battles, including Elkhorn Tavern (Pea Ridge) in Arkansas in early March 1862. There, his men captured several Union artillery pieces, but the atrocities committed against white soldiers, including scalping, were used by the press to demonize Native American participation in the war. Watie led his men in dozens of small actions over a sprawling region. When he finally surrendered in June of 1865, it is believed he was the last general to officially do so. He died in 1871 and is buried in the Old Ridge Cemetery in Delaware County, Oklahoma.

Literally scores of skirmishes and larger actions were fought on the land running from west of the Mississippi all the way to the New Mexico Territory. While the federal government was fighting to control the Apache in the New Mexico Territory, significant fighting broke out between major tribes over land rights, hunting issues, cultural matters, and traditional rivalries. The fact that some tribes aligned themselves with the Federal government while others threw their lot in with the Confederacy only served to fan the flames of hatred. As Indian fought Indian, other more famous actions broke out across the country.

The Dakota War, in the summer of 1862 in Minnesota, was a short but brutal affair that began in August between eastern Sioux or Dakota and white settlers and Union troops. The fighting was put down within a short time, and the affair ended with the mass hanging of thirty-eight Dakota that December in Mankato, Minnesota. Because many of the white soldiers were shipped elsewhere to fight in the main civil war, Indians in Colorado used the occasion to launch hit-and-run raids against farmers and ranchers outside Denver. In an effort to end the threat, Colonel John Chivington led nearly 1,000 volunteers in a punitive expedition that attacked a village with hundreds of Arapaho and Cheyenne, including women and children. Chivington refused to take prisoners, which explains why the fighting is commonly called the Sand Creek Massacre.

Because Indian Territory was so far from the Confederate capital in Richmond, Virginia, Southern authorities dedicated fewer resources and capable officers to supply and oversee it. It was also hard to transfer men and supplies across the Mississippi River, especially after the fall of Vicksburg and Port Hudson in the summer of 1863. The result was that pro-Confederate Indians found it increasingly difficult to battle Federal expeditions and raids.

Native Americans who sided with the South suffered the most for their allegiance. All existing Federal treaties with Indian tribes who sided with the South were voided. Despite its efforts to enlist Indians, the Confederacy garnered few military benefits from its relationship with them.

Glossary of Civil War Terms

Abatis: a defensive work consisting of a series of felled trees, their ends sharpened and pointed toward the enemy.

Abolitionist: a person who advocated the abolishment, or ending, of slavery.

Anaconda Plan: U.S. General Winfield Scott's strategic plan to quell the rebellion, which called for a blockade of southern ports and occupation of the Mississippi River—surrounding and squeezing the Confederate states into submission like a giant snake, or anaconda.

Antebellum: From the Latin *ante* (before) and *bellum* (war), refers to the period preceding the Civil War.

Artillery: a term used to describe large-caliber guns, or cannon, as well as the branch of service that operated such weapons.

Blue Belly: Confederate term—derived from the slang 'yellowbelly,' or coward—for Union soldiers.

Bounty: money paid by states and the federal government to entice men to enlist in the Union armed forces. Bounties ranged from $300.00 to over $700.00.

Bounty Jumper: someone who joined the Union armed forces, collected an enlistment bounty, deserted, and repeated the process. Some "Bounty Jumpers" joined as many as half-a-dozen units during the course of the war.

Breastwork: : a temporary defensive work erected to protect troops from enemy fire; often constructed in haste out of available materials, such as earth and felled trees.

Brevet: a temporary or honorary rank, often granted for meritorious service during war, which did not carry the authority or pay of a full rank.

Caisson: a house-drawn wagon or chest designed to carry ammunition for field artillery.

Canister: an artillery projectile consisting of small iron or lead balls packed with sawdust into a tin can, or canister. The balls scattered upon firing, acting like a shotgun blast. Normally utilized against attacking infantry, canister rounds had an effective range of 100 to 400 yards.

Carpetbaggers: Northerners who flocked to the South during Reconstruction in search of financial gain. The term derived from the carpetbags in which such men often carried their belongings.

Chevaux-de-frise: a wooden frame (often a single log) embedded with crossed wooden spikes, pointed toward the enemy. Often used to fill gaps in a defensive line.

Christian Commission: a massive volunteer organization that provided aid to soldiers during the war, from reading material to medical supplies and treatment.

Commutation: the process of drafted men paying a fee (often $300.00) to avoid military service.

Contrabands: term used to describe fugitive slaves who came into Union lines during the war. U.S. officials considered these ex-slaves contrabands of war because their labor aided the Southern war effort.

Copperheads: Northern Democrats opposed to the war. Also referred to as "Peace Democrats," they advocated an immediate peace settlement with the Confederacy. Many were imprisoned after Abraham Lincoln suspended the right of *habeas corpus*.

Defilade: a position protected, via natural or manmade barrier, from enemy fire or observation.

Demonstration: a secondary or threatened attack designed to deceive the enemy. Demonstrations were made against a portion of the enemy's line away from the target of the main attack.

Earthwork: a defensive work erected to protect troops from enemy fire; often consisting of a series of trenches.

Emancipation Proclamation: Presidential order, preliminarily issued September 22, 1862, freeing all slaves in states still in rebellion as of January 1, 1863. Slaves in the border states (Delaware, Kentucky, Maryland, Missouri) were exempted. Paved the way for ex-slaves to enter the U.S. Army and Navy.

Enfilade: gunfire directed along an enemy's battle line from a flanking position, producing maximum damage with minimum exposure.

Flank: the end of an army's line in battle, or a type of attack directed at an enemy's flank (i.e., a flanking maneuver).

Furlough: leave granted enlisted men, often those sick or wounded, to return home for a period of time.

Galvanized Yankees: Confederate prisoners of war who swore allegiance to the United States and joined the Union army. The six regiments of Galvanized Yankees raised were sent west to fight Indians.

Grand Army of the Republic: the politically powerful fraternal organization of Union veterans of the war, founded in 1866. Often referred to as 'the GAR.'

Grape Shot: an artillery projectile consisting of a number of iron balls held together by iron plates and rings. Largely superceded by canister by the start of the war.

Greybacks: 1. Lice.

2. Union troops' slang term for Confederates, derived from their grey uniforms.

Guerrilla: a term for civilians who engaged in warfare, or for the hit-and-run tactics they employed.

Hardtack: a hard wheat biscuit, 3 by 3 inches, issued as rations to troops, who regularly derided it as inedible.

Haversack: a small, durable bag in which soldiers carried personal belongings; often slung over one shoulder.

Invalid Corps: a reserve command established in 1863 consisting of Union soldiers (both on active service or recently discharged) too disabled to serve in combat but capable of performing other light military duties (e.g., provost guard, nursing, cooking, garrison duty). Renamed the Veterans Reserve Corps (VRC) in 1864, over 60,000 men served in its ranks during the war.

Ironclad: a warship covered (clad) with iron plating; all Civil War ironclads were steam powered.

Legion: a regiment consisting of infantry, cavalry, and artillery companies.

Minie Ball: a cone-shaped lead bullet, designed by and named after Captain Claude-Etienne Minié of the French army, used in rifled muskets. The bullet's hollow base expanded upon firing, forcing it into the grooves (or rifling) inside the gun's barrel. As a result, the bullet spun as it exited the barrel, stabilizing it in flight and resulting in increased range and accuracy.

Mortar: a large but short-barreled artillery piece designed to lob explosive shells at a high arc toward enemy positions. Used most often during siege operations. The war's largest mortar, called the *Dictator*, sent 200-pound explosive shells a distance of approximately 2 ½ miles.

Parole: status of prisoners of war released on their personal assurance that they would not again take up arms until formally exchanged.

Picket: a soldier on guard, often beyond the main lines. A group of pickets, or a picket line, was often employed to guard against a surprise enemy attack.

Pontoon: a low, flat-bottomed wooden boat. Pontoon bridges—dozens to hundreds of pontoons strung together and covered with wooden boards—allowed advancing armies to cross various bodies of water in short order.

Quaker Gun: a log painted to resemble a cannon to fool the enemy. The name apparently stemmed from the Quakers' opposition to war.

Ram: a stream-powered boat with an iron ram attached to its bow, designed to sink enemy ships via collision.

Reconstruction: term for the immediate postwar period (1865-1877), during which the federal government grappled with issues surrounding reconciliation and race in the former Confederate states.

Sanitary Commission: a federal government agency created in 1861 to coordinate the volunteer efforts of women during the war. Female volunteers organized fundraisers, staffed hospitals, and sewed uniforms, among countless other activities.

Scalawag: a white southerner who supported Republican efforts during Reconstruction.

Secesh: shorthand for "secessionist," a person who advocated the secession of southern states in 1860-1861 or supported the Confederate war effort.

Siege: military tactic by which an enemy force is surrounded, preventing its re-supply and forcing it into eventual surrender.

Skedaddle: slang word, often employed by soldiers, referring to a hasty withdrawal or retreat.

Skirmish: light combat, often entailing an exchange of fire between opposing pickets or other advanced forces.

Sutler: a civilian merchant authorized to sell miscellaneous goods (e.g., tobacco, books, food) to soldiers. Sutlers followed the armies in horse-drawn carts, setting up shop when the armies camped.

Torpedo: name describing any one of a variety of exploding mines employed during the war, both on land and in sea.

USCT: United States Colored Troops, regiments of the U.S. Army that consisted of black soldiers and white officers.

Veterans Reserve Corps: see Invalid Corps.

Zouave: a member of a Union or Confederate regiment patterned after the French Zouaves and distinguished by their colorful uniforms, including baggy trousers and turbans or fezzes.

Civil War Points of Interest

Whether searching for a Civil War related locale in your area or planning an extended Civil War themed trip, the following list of sites will get you started. All contact information—including Web sites, where available—was current at the time of publication. Operating hours vary, so please check ahead before hitting the road.

ALABAMA

Confederate Memorial Park
437 County Road 63
Marbury, Alabama 36051
(205) 755-1990
http://www.800alabama.com/things-to-do/alabama-attractions/confederate_memo rial_park.html
Two cemeteries and a museum tell the story of Alabama's Confederate Soldiers' Home.

Fort Gaines Historical Site
51 Bienville Boulevard
Dauphin Island, Alabama 36528
(251) 861-6992
http://www.dauphinisland.org/fort.htm
Fort Gaines protected Mobile Bay from Union attack during the Civil War.

Fort Morgan State Historic Site
51 Highway 180 West
Gulf Shores, AL 36542
(334) 540-7125
Visitors can view the bay through which Admiral David Farragut's fleet passed during the Battle of Mobile Bay.

ARKANSAS

Arkansas Post National Memorial
1741 Old Post Road
Gillett, AR 72055
870-548-2207
http://www.nps.gov/arpo/index.htm

Preserves the site of Fort Hindman, constructed by Confederates in 1862 and captured by Federal forces in 1863. The earthen structure has since been destroyed by erosion.

Jenkins' Ferry State Park
Located 13 miles south of Sheridan on Ark. 46
http://www.arkansasstateparks.com/park-finder/parks.aspx?id=28
(No staff on site.)
Federal troops, retreating after the failed Red River Campaign, beat off Confederate attacks and crossed the Saline River here on April 30, 1864.

Marks' Mills State Park
Located southeast of Fordyce at the junction of Ark. 97 and Ark. 8.
888-AT-PARKS
http://www.arkansasstateparks.com/marksmills/
During the Red River Campaign in April 1864, Confederates captured 210-wagon Union supply train.

Pea Ridge National Military Park
15930 E Highway 62
Garfield, AR 72732
(479) 451-8122
http://www.nps.gov/peri/
Several thousand Native Americans fought with the Confederate army at Elkhorn Tavern (Pea Ridge). U.S. forces won the battle, keeping Missouri in the Union.

Poison Spring State Park
Located 10 miles west of Camden on Ark. 76
888-AT-PARKS
http://www.arkansasstateparks.com/poisonspring/
A Red River Campaign spot at which Confederates ambushed a Union supply train, capturing 198 wagons loaded with corn.

Praire Grove Battlefield State Park
506 East Douglas Street
Prairie Grove, AR 72753
(479) 846-2990
http://www.arkansasstateparks.com/prairiegrovebattlefield/
This December 1862 battle was the last major engagement fought in northeastern Arkansas.

COLORADO

Sand Creek Massacre National Historic Site
35110 Highway 194 E.

La Junta, CO 81050
(719) 438-5916
http://www.nps.gov/sand/index.htm
In late November 1864, soldiers under Colonel John Chivington attacked Cheyenne Chief Black Kettle's village, slaughtering over 150 women and children.

DISTRICT OF COLUMBIA

Ford's Theatre National Historical Site
511 10th Street NW
Washington DC 20004
(202) 233-0701
http://www.nps.gov/foth/
John Wilkes Booth assassinated Abraham Lincoln here on April 14, 1865. The president died the next morning, across the street in the Petersen House.

Fort Circle Parks
Located at various sites in and around the city
http://www.nps.gov/cwdw/index.htm
Visitors can view the locations and remnants of a number of the forts erected to defend the capital during the war.

Lincoln's Cottage at the Soldiers' Home
Washington, DC 20011-8400
(202) 829-0436
http://www.lincolncottage.org/index.htm (See website for directions)
Lincoln and his family resided here for significant stretches of time during the war.

FLORIDA

Gulf Islands National Seashore - Gulf Breeze
1801 Gulf Breeze Parkway
Gulf Breeze, FL 32563
(850) 934-2600
http://www.nps.gov/guis/index.htm
Civil War-era forts Barrancas, Pickens, Massachusetts, and McRee are located within the park.

Natural Bridge Battlefield Historic State Park
7502 Natural Bridge Road
Tallahassee, Florida 32305
(850) 922-6007

http://www.floridastateparks.org/naturalbridge/default.cfm
Confederates turned back a Federal advance here on March 6, 1865.

Olustee Battlefield Historic State Park
P. O. Box 40
Olustee, Florida 32072
(386) 758-0400
http://www.floridastateparks.org/olustee/default.cfm
Site of the February 1864 battle in which several U.S. Colored Troops regiments participated.

GEORGIA

Andersonville National Historic Site
496 Cemetery Road
Andersonville, GA 31711
(229) 924-0343
http://www.nps.gov/ande/
Site of the largest Confederate-run POW camp, in which over 12,000 Union soldiers perished.

Chickamauga and Chattanooga National Military Park
P.O. Box 2128
Fort Oglethorpe, Georgia 30742
(706) 866-9241
http://www.nps.gov/chch/
The nation's first national military park preserves the site of the last major Confederate victory of the war.

Fort McAllister Historic Park
3894 Fort McAllister Road
Richmond Hill, GA 31324
(912) 727-2339
http://gastateparks.org/info/ftmcallister/
The Confederate garrison at Fort McAllister, located south of Savannah, beat off seven attacks by enemy warships before falling to Union ground forces in 1864.

Fort Pulaski National Monument - Tybee Island
P. O. Box 30757
Savannah, GA 31410
(912) 786-5787
http://www.nps.gov/fopu/

Considered invincible, Fort Pulaski guarded the water approach to Savannah. In April 1862, U.S. rifled cannon battered the fort into submission in less than two days.

Jefferson Davis Memorial Historic Site
338 Jeff Davis Park Rd
Fitzgerald, GA 31750
(229) 831-2335
http://www.gastateparks.org/info/jeffd/
A monument and museum mark the site were Union forces captured the Confederate president on May 9, 1865.

Kennesaw Mountain National Battlefield Park
900 Kennesaw Mountain Dr.
Kennesaw, GA 30152
(770) 427-4686
http://www.nps.gov/kemo/
At Kennesaw Mountain, Confederates foiled General William T. Sherman's attempt to break their lines during the campaign for Atlanta.

Pickett's Mill Battlefield Historic Site
4432 Mt. Tabor Church Rd
Dallas, GA 30157
(770) 443-7850
http://www.gastateparks.org/info/picketts/
This park, the site of a Confederate victory on May 27, 1864, is one of the few preserved fields of a major engagement near Atlanta.

ILLINOIS

Lincoln Home National Historic Site
413 South Eighth Street
Springfield, Illinois 62701-1905
(217) 391-3226
http://www.nps.gov/liho/
Lincoln lived here from 1844 until he left for Washington in 1861.

INDIANA

Lincoln Boyhood National Memorial
2916 E. South Street
Lincoln City, IN 47552
(812) 937-4541
http://www.nps.gov/libo/
An interpretive site devoted to Lincoln's formative years in Indiana.

KANSAS

Fort Scott National Historic Site
P.O. Box 918
Fort Scott, KS 66701
(620) 223-0310
http://www.nps.gov/fosc
Fort Scott served as a Union supply depot during the war.

John Brown State Historic Site
10th and Main Street
Osawatomie, Kansas 66064
(913) 755-4384
http://www.kshs.org/places/johnbrown/index.htm
View the cabin where abolitionist John Brown fought pro-slavery militia in 1856.

Mine Creek Battlefield State Historic Site
20485 Kansas Highway 52
Pleasanton, KS 66075
(913) 352-8890
http://www.kshs.org/places/minecreek/index.htm
On October 25, 1864, outnumbered Union cavalry defeated their counterparts at Mine Creek, capturing roughly 600 Confederates, including two generals.

Marais des Cygnes State Historic Site
20485 Kansas Highway 52
Pleasanton, KS 66075
(913) 352-8890
http://www.kshs.org/places/marais/index.htm
Visitors can tour the site of the murder of five free-state settlers by proslavery settlers during the "Bleeding Kansas" era.

KENTUCKY

Abraham Lincoln Birthplace National Historic Site
2995 Lincoln Farm Road
Hodgenville, KY 42748
(270) 358-3137
http://www.nps.gov/abli/index.htm
Abraham Lincoln was born here on February 12, 1809.

Columbus-Belmont State Park
350 Park Road
Columbus, KY 42032

(270) 677-2327
http://parks.ky.gov/findparks/recparks/cb/
U.S. Grant, in his first battle as a Union general, defeated Confederates at Belmont in November 1861.

Jefferson Davis Monument State Historic Site
Highway 68 E
Fairview, KY 42221
(270) 889-6100
http://parks.ky.gov/findparks/histparks/jd/
Jefferson Davis' birth place (June 3, 1808).

Perryville Battlefield State Historic Site
1825 Battlefield Road
Perryville, KY 40468-0296
859-332-8631
http://parks.ky.gov/findparks/histparks/pb/
The decisive Battle of Perryville ended Braxton Bragg's 1862 invasion of Kentucky, keeping the state in the Union.

LOUISIANA

Camp Moore Confederate Cemetery and Museum
Hwy. 51
Tangipahoa, LA 70465
(985) 229-2438
http://personal.atl.bellsouth.net/c/o/cosby_w/
Camp Moore was Louisiana's largest Civil War training camp.

Centenary State Historic Site
3522 College St.
Jackson, LA 70748
(888) 677-2364
http://www.crt.state.la.us/parks/icentenary.aspx
Centenary College closed during the war, and both sides utilized its vacant buildings (as hospital space and headquarters).

Fort Pike State Historic Site
27100 Chef Menteur Highway
New Orleans, LA 70129
(504) 255-9171
http://www.crt.state.la.us/parks/iFortpike.aspx
Confederates abandoned the fort when Federal troops took New Orleans. Under Union control, the fort became a training ground for members of USCT regiments.

Mansfield State Historic Site
15149 Highway 175
Mansfield, LA 71052
318-872-1474
http://www.crt.state.la.us/parks/iMansfld.aspx
This Confederate victory halted Nathaniel P. Banks' Red River Expedition.

Port Hudson State Historic Site
236 Hwy. 61
Jackson, LA 70748
(225) 654-3775
http://www.crt.state.la.us/parks/ipthudson.aspx
Port Hudson, the last Confederate stronghold on the Mississippi River, surrendered after a 48-day siege, just a short time after Vicksburg fell.

MARYLAND

Antietam National Battlefield
P.O. Box 158
Sharpsburg, MD 21782
(301) 432-5124
http://www.nps.gov/anti/
The Battle of Antietam (Sharpsburg), the bloodiest single day of the war, marked the end of Robert E. Lee's first raid into the North.

Clara Barton National Historic Site
5801 Oxford Road
Glen Echo, Maryland 20812
(301) 320-1410
http://www.nps.gov/clba/
Visitors can tour the home of Clara Barton, Civil War nurse and founder of the American Red Cross.

Fort Washington Park
13551 Fort Washington Road
Fort Washington, Maryland 20744
(301) 763-4600
http://www.nps.gov/fowa/index.htm
Fort Washington was one of many that guarded Washington D.C. during the war.

Gathland State Park
21843 National Pike
Boonsboro, MD 21713
(301) 791-4767

http://www.dnr.state.md.us/publiclands/western/gathland.html
The park protects much of the site of the 1862 fight for South Mountain, a precursor to the Battle of Antietam.

Monocacy National Battlefield
5201 Urbana Pike
Frederick, MD 21704
(301) 662-3515
http://www.nps.gov/mono/
The engagement at Monocacy, known as "the battle that saved Washington," occurred during Confederate General Jubal Early's advance toward the capital in the summer of 1864.

National Museum of Civil War Medicine
48 E. Patrick Street
Frederick, MD 21705-0470
301-695-1864
http://www.civilwarmed.org/
Visitors interested in the medical side of the war will enjoy the museum's many programs and exhibits.

MISSISSIPPI

Beauvoir
The Jefferson Davis Home and Presidential Library
2244 Beach Blvd.
Biloxi, MS 39531
(228) 388-4400
http://www.beauvoir.org/
Davis' final home was used as a Confederate Veterans Home between 1903 and 1957.

Brices Cross Roads National Battlefield Site
Located on Mississippi 370 near Baldwyn, Mississippi.
http://www.nps.gov/brcr/
On June 10, 1864, Major General Nathan Bedford Forrest's 3,500-man cavalry corps routed General Samuel D. Sturgis' 8,100 Union troops. The city of Baldwyn operates a visitors center near the battlefield. For more information on this action, see http://www.bricescrossroads.com

Corinth Civil War Interpretive Center (a unit of Shiloh National Military Park)
Museum and Visitor Center (662) 287-9273
Commemorates the battle and Siege of Corinth (April 29 - June 10, 1862), and Second Battle of Corinth (October 3-4, 1862).
Grand Gulf Military Park

12006 Grand Gulf Road
Port Gibson, MS 39150
(601) 437-5911
http://www.grandgulfpark.state.ms.us/
The Confederate battery at Grand Gulf drove off Rear Admiral David D. Porter's ironclads, thwarting U.S. Grant's plans to land troops there.

Natchez National Historical Park
640 South Canal Street, Box E
Natchez, MS 39120
601-446-5790
http://www.nps.gov/natc/
Commemorates life in the antebellum South and slavery.

Tupelo National Battlefield
Located on Main Street in Tupelo, Mississippi.
http://www.nps.gov/tupe/
Federal troops beat back multiple Confederate attacks during this 1864 battle. There is no visitor center. For more information, contact Natchez Trace Parkway Visitor Center: (800) 305-7417

Vicksburg National Military Park
3201 Clay Street
Vicksburg, MS 39183-3495
(601) 636-0583
http://www.nps.gov/vick/
U.S. Grant's siege and capture of Vicksburg helped split the Confederacy in two, opening the Mississippi River to Union shipping.

MISSOURI

Battle of Athens State Historic Site
Route 1, Box 26, Hwy. CC
Revere, MO 63465
(660) 877-3871
http://www.mostateparks.com/athens.htm
The site of the northernmost Civil War battle fought west of the Mississippi.

Battle of Lexington State Historic Site
1101 Delaware Street
Lexington, MO 64067
(660) 259-4654
http://www.mostateparks.com/lexington/index.html

The restored Anderson House still shows damage inflicted by cannon balls fired during the "Battle of the Hemp Bales."

Confederate Memorial State Historic Site
211 West First Street
Higginsville, MO 64037
(660) 584-2853
http://www.mostateparks.com/confedmem.htm
Although Missouri remained in the Union, many of its residents fought for the Confederacy. The Confederate Soldiers Home of Missouri opened in 1891 and housed more than 1,600 Confederate veterans and their families over six decades of operation.

Ulysses S Grant National Historic Site
7400 Grant Road
St. Louis, MO 63123
(314) 842-3298
http://www.nps.gov/ulsg/
Visitors can tour "White Haven," the childhood home of Grant's wife, Julia Dent, where the couple lived in the 1850s.

Wilson's Creek National Battlefield
6424 West Farm Road 182
Republic, MO 65738
(417) 732-2662 /
http://www.nps.gov/wicr/
The Confederates won this 1861 battle, in which Union General Nathaniel Lyon met his death.

NEW MEXICO

Pecos National Historical Park
P. O. Box 418
Pecos, NM 87552-0418
(505) 757-7200
http://www.nps.gov/peco/
The 1862 Battle of Glorieta Pass marked the end of Rebel occupation of New Mexico.

NORTH CAROLINA

Bennett Place
4409 Bennett Memorial Rd.
Durham, NC 27705
(919) 383-4345

http://www.nchistoricsites.org/Bennett/Bennett.htm
This restored farmhouse was the site of the surrender of General Joseph Johnston's
Confederate army.

Bentonville Battlefield
5466 Harper House Road
Four Oaks, NC 27524
(910) 594-0789
http://www.nchistoricsites.org/Bentonvi/Bentonvi.HTM
Bentonville was the final Confederate attempt to stop Sherman's advance through
North Carolina.

CSS *Neuse* State Historic Site
2612 W. Vernon Ave.
Kinston, NC 28504
(252) 522-2091
www.nchistoricsites.org/neuse/neuse.htm
Displays remnants of the salvaged ironclad gunboat CSS *Neuse*.

Fort Fisher
P.O. Box 169
Kure Beach, NC 28449
(910) 458-5538
http://www.nchistoricsites.org/fisher/fisher.htm
Fort Fisher fell on January 15, 1865, closing the South's last port in Wilmington, NC.

Fort Macon State Park
2300 East Fort Macon Road
Atlantic Beach, NC 28512
(252) 726-3775
http://www.ncparks.gov/Visit/parks/foma/main.php
Confederates seized this fort in 1861, and Union troops took it back in 1862.

PENNSYLVANIA

Gettysburg National Military Park
1195 Baltimore Pike
Gettysburg, PA 17325
(717) 334-1124
http://www.nps.gov/gett/
The three-day battle at Gettysburg ended Robert E. Lee's second invasion of the
North. The new and enlarged Vistors' Center is a must-see.

National Civil War Museum
One Lincoln Circle at Reservoir Park
P.O. Box 1861
Harrisburg, PA 17105-1861
(717) 260-1861
http://www.nationalcivilwarmuseum.org/
A variety of exhibits tell the story of the war.

SOUTH CAROLINA

Fort Sumter Visitor Education Center
340 Concord Street
Charleston, SC 29401
http://www.nps.gov/fosu
The visitor education center's extensive collections shed light on the causes of the war and its outbreak at Fort Sumter in April 1861. The fort is a separate entity, accessible only by ferry.

Rivers Bridge State Historic Site
325 State Park Rd.
Ehrhardt, SC 29081
(803) 267-3675
http://www.southcarolinaparks.com/park-finder/state-park/566.aspx
For two days in early February 1865, outnumbered Confederates slowed Sherman's march through South Carolina at River's Bridge.

TENNESSEE

Carnton Plantation
1345 Carnton Lane
Franklin, TN 37064
(615) 794-0903
http://www.carnton.org/
The November 1864 Battle of Franklin swirled around John McGavock's plantation home, which afterward served as a field hospital. After the war, the McGavock family put aside land to serve as a cemetery, in which some 1,500 Confederates are buried.

Carter House
1140 Columbia Ave
Franklin, TN 37065
(615) 791-1861
http://www.carterhouse1864.com/

This state-owned site preserves Confederate General John B. Hood's disastrous attack on General John M. Schofield's Union army.

Chickamauga / Chattanooga National Military Park - Lookout Mountain Unit
P.O. Box 2128
Fort Oglethorpe, Georgia 30742
(706) 866-9241
http://www.nps.gov/chch/
After defeating William S. Rosecrans' Federals at Chickamauga, Confederate General Braxton Bragg laid siege to Chattanooga. Grant replaced Rosecrans and drove Bragg's army from its positions. (See also the entry under Georgia for contact information.)

Fort Donelson National Battlefield
P.O. Box 434
Dover, TN 37058
(931) 232-5348
http://www.nps.gov/fodo/index.htm
When Fort Donelson's Confederate commander asked Union General U.S. Grant for surrender terms, Grant replied: "No terms except an unconditional and immediate surrender can be accepted." The loss of Donelson opened Tennessee to invasion.

Fort Pillow State Historic Park
3122 Park Road
Henning, TN 38041
(731) 738-5581
http://www.tennessee.gov/environment/parks/FortPillow/
On April 12, 1864, Major General Nathan Bedford Forrest's Confederates overran the Union fort, killing 350 troops, many of them black, in an event regarded as a massacre.

Johnsonville State Historic Park
90 Redoubt Lane
New Johnsonville, TN 37134
(931) 535-2789
http://www.tennessee.gov/environment/parks/Johnsonville/
On November 4, 1864, Nathan Bedford Forrest's Confederate cavalry raided Johnsonvile, capturing four Union gunboats and 14 steamboats.

Shiloh National Military Park
1055 Pittsburg Landing Road
Shiloh, Tennessee 38376
(731) 689-5696
http://www.nps.gov/shil/
A Union victory, the two-day battle at Shiloh witnessed the death of the Confederate commander, Albert Sidney Johnston. The park is nearly pristine, and is the finest example we have of a major preserved Civil War battlefield.

Stones River National Battlefield
3501 Old Nashville Highway
Murfreesboro, TN 37129
(615) 893-9501
http://www.nps.gov/stri/
The Federal victory at Stones River drove Braxton Bragg's Confederate army from its winter quarters.

TEXAS

Sabine Pass Battleground State Historic Site
6100 Dowling Road
Port Arthur, Texas 77640
(512) 463-6323
http://www.thc.state.tx.us/hsites/hs_sabine.aspx?Site=Sabine
A bronze statue of Lieutenant Dick Dowling marks the site where he and his 46 Confederates drove off four Union gunboats and seven troop transports, saving East Texas from invasion.

VIRGINIA

Appomattox Court House National Historical Park
P.O. Box 218
Appomattox, VA 24522
(434) 352-8987
http://www.nps.gov/apco/index.htm
Visitors to the park can view the reconstructed McLean House, where Robert E. Lee surrendered to U.S. Grant in April 1865.

Arlington House, The Robert E. Lee Memorial
The Arlington House is located in Arlington National Cemetery.
Call (703) 235-1530 for information.
http://www.nps.gov/arho/index.htm
Arlington was Robert E. Lee's home for over 30 years. In 1861, the Lees fled south, never to return.

Cedar Creek & Belle Grove National Historical Park - Middletown and Strasburg
For more information, call the park's office at (540) 868-9176.
http://www.nps.gov/cebe/index.htm
This new National Historic Park is in development. Visitors can visit two privately owned sites: Belle Grove Plantation and the Cedar Creek Battlefield Visitor Center.

Fredericksburg & Spotsylvania National Military Park
120 Chatham Lane
Fredericksburg, Virginia 22405
(540) 373-6122
http://www.nps.gov/frsp/index.htm
This park preserves parts of four major Civil War battles: Fredericksburg, Chancellorsville, the Wilderness, and Spotsylvania Court House.

Manassas National Battlefield Park
12521 Lee Highway
Manassas, VA 20109-2005
(703) 361-1339
http://www.nps.gov/mana/index.htm
The Confederates won the Battle of First Manassas in July 1861. A year later, the armies met on the same ground, and the Confederates prevailed a second time.

Museum and White House of the Confederacy
1201 E. Clay Street
Richmond, VA 23219
(804) 649-1861
http://www.moc.org/site/PageServer/
The museum holds one of the largest collections of Confederate artifacts in the country. It is currently considering breaking up its collection into several museum locations across the state, including one at Appomattox.

Petersburg National Battlefield
1539 Hickory Hill Road
Petersburg, VA 23803
(804) 732-3531
http://www.nps.gov/pete/index.htm
The 292-day Union siege of Petersburg-Richmond cost some 20,000 Confederates their lives.

Richmond National Battlefield Park
3215 East Broad Street
Richmond, VA 23223
(804) 226-1981
http://www.nps.gov/rich/index.htm
Visitors can tour sites from both the 1862 and 1864 Union attempts to capture Richmond, the capital of the Confederacy.

Sailor's Creek Battlefield State Park
6888 Green Bay Rd.
Green Bay, VA 23942

(this is a mailing address, not a physical location)
(434) 315-0349
http://www.dcr.virginia.gov/state_parks/sai.shtml
Philip Sheridan's Union cavalry cut off about one-fourth of Lee's retreating army here in April 1865. Over 7,700 Confederates surrendered, including eight generals.

Staunton River Bridge
The park has two visitor centers.
Call (434) 454-4312 for directions.
http://www.stauntonriverbattlefield.org/
On June 25, 1864, 492 old men and young boys helped 296 Confederate reserves defeat over 5,000 Union cavalrymen.

WEST VIRGINIA

Carnifex Ferry Battlefield State Park
1194 Carnifex Ferry Rd.
Summersville, WV 26651
(304) 872-0825
http://www.carnifexferrybattlefieldstatepark.com/
Union forces retained control of the Kanawha Valley after their victory in 1861.

Droop Mountain Battlefield State Park
HC 64 Box 189
Hillsboro, WV 24946
http://www.droopmountainbattlefield.com/
The Union victory at Droop Mountain ended Confederate operations in West Virginia.

Harpers Ferry National Historical Park
P.O. Box 65
Harpers Ferry, WV 25425
(304) 535-6029
http://www.nps.gov/hafe/index.htm
Harpers Ferry was the site of John Brown's raid (1859) and the largest surrender of Union troops during the war (1862).

Civil War Bookshelf

By no means comprehensive, the following list aims to provide casual readers (serious buffs are already well familiar with these titles) with a number of ideas for additional reading on a variety of Civil War subjects. If you have an interest in building a balanced Civil War collection, this list is a good way to begin. (Note that many of the older titles have been reprinted.)

General Histories:

Foote, Shelby, *The Civil War: A Narrative* 3 vols. (1958-1974)

Johnson, Robert and Buel, Clarence, eds., *Battles and Leaders of the Civil War* 4 vols. (1887-1888)

McPherson, James, *Battle Cry of Freedom: The Civil War Era* (1988)

Battles and Campaigns:

Coddington, Edwin B., *The Gettysburg Campaign: A Study in Command* (1968)

Cunningham, O. Edward, Gary D. Joiner and Timothy B. Smith (eds.), *Shiloh and the Western Campaign of 1862* (2006)

Daniel, Larry J., *Shiloh: The Battle That Changed the Civil War* (1997)

Gottfried, Bradley M., *The Maps of Gettysburg* (2007)

———, *The Maps of First Bull Run (Manassas)* (2009)

Petruzzi, J. David, and Stanley, Steven, *The Complete Gettysburg Guide* (2009)

Rable, George C., *Fredericksburg! Fredericksburg!* (2001)

Rhea, Gordon C., *The Battle of the Wilderness, May 5-6, 1864* (1994)

———, *To the North Anna River: Grant and Lee, May 13-25, 1864* (2000)

———, *Cold Harbor: Grant and Lee, May 26-June 5, 1864* (2002)

Sears, Stephen W., *Gettysburg* (2003)

———, *Landscape Turned Red: The Battle of Antietam* (1983)

———, *To the Gates of Richmond: The Peninsula Campaign* (1992)

Shea, William L. and Winschel, Terrence J., *Vicksburg is the Key: The Struggle for the Mississippi River* (2003)

Smith, Timothy B., *Champion Hill: Decisive Battle for Vicksburg* (2004)

Wittenberg, Eric, Petruzzi, J. David, and Nugent, Michael F. *One Continuous Fight: The Retreat from Gettysburg and the Pursuit of Lee's Army of Northern Virginia, July 4-14, 1863* (2008)

Woodworth, Stephen E., *Six Armies in Tennessee: The Chickamauga and Chattanooga Campaigns* (1998)

The Armies

Beatie, Russel H. *Army of the Potomac*, 3 vols. to date. (2002 - 2008)

Catton, Bruce, *Bruce Catton's Civil War: Three Volumes in One (Mr. Lincoln's Army, Glory Road, A Stillness at Appomattox)* (1984)

Connelly, Thomas Lawrence, *Army of the Heartland: The Army of Tennessee, 1861-1862* (1967)

———, *Autumn of Glory: The Army of Tennessee, 1862-1865* (1971)

Daniel, Larry J., *Days of Glory: The Army of the Cumberland, 1861-1865* (2004)

Glatthaar, Joseph T., *General Lee's Army: From Victory to Collapse* (2008)

Power, J. Tracy, *Lee's Miserables: Life in the Army of Northern Virginia from the Wilderness to Appomattox* (2002)

Prokopowicz, Gerald J., *All for the Regiment: The Army of the Ohio, 1861-1862* (2000)

Rafuse, Ethan, *Robert E. Lee and the Fall of the Confederacy, 1863-1865* (2008)

Wert, Jeffry D., *The Sword of Lincoln: The Army of the Potomac* (2006)

Woodworth, Steven E., *Nothing But Victory: The Army of the Tennessee, 1861-1865* (2005)

Commanders

Collins, Darrell, *Major General Robert E Rodes of the Army of Northern Virginia* (2008)

Freeman, Douglas, *Lee's Lieutenants: A Study in Command* 3 vols. (1943)

Glatthaar, Joseph T., *Partners in Command: The Relationships Between Leaders in the Civil War* (1994)

Grant, Ulysses S., *Personal Memoirs of Ulysses S. Grant* (1885)

McFeely, William S., *Grant: A Biography* (2002)

Marszalek, John F., *Sherman: A Soldier's Passion for Order* (1992)

Nolan, Alan T., *Lee Considered: General Robert E. Lee and Civil War History* (1991)

Robertson, James I. Jr., *Stonewall Jackson: The Man, the Soldier, the Legend* (1997)

Royster, Charles, *The Destructive War: William Tecumseh Sherman, Stonewall Jackson, and the Americans* (1991)

Sears, Stephen W., *George B. McClellan: The Young Napoleon* (1988)

Thomas, Emory, *Robert E. Lee: A Biography* (1995)

Wert, Jeffry D., *General James Longstreet: The Confederacy's Most Controversial Soldier* (1993)

Regimental / Unit Histories

Caldwell, J.F.J. *The History of a Brigade of South Carolinians* (1951)

Davis, William C. *The Orphan Brigade: The Kentucky Confederates Who Couldn't Go Home* (1983)

Gannon, James P. *Irish Rebels, Confederate Tigers: The 6th Louisiana Volunteers, 1861-1865* (1999)

Hess, Earl J. *Lee's Tar Heels: The Pettigrew–Kirkland–MacRae Brigade* (2001)

Miller, Richard F., *Harvard's Civil War: A History of the Twentieth Massachusetts Volunteer Infantry* (2005)

Moe, Richard, *The Last Full Measure: The Life and Death of the First Minnesota Volunteers* (1993)

Pullen, John J., *The Twentieth Maine: A Volunteer Regiment in the Civil War* (1957)

Wilkinson, Warren, *Mother, May You Never See the Sights I've Seen: The Fifty-Seventh Massachusetts Veteran Volunteers in the Army of the Potomac, 1864-1865* (1990)

Soldiers and Soldiering

Daniel, Larry J., *Soldiering in the Army of Tennessee: A Portrait of Life in a Confederate Army* (1991)

Glatthaar, Joseph T., *The March to the Sea and Beyond: Sherman's Troops in the Savannah and Carolinas Campaigns* (1985)

Herdegen, Lance J. *"Those Damned Black Hats!" The Iron Brigade in the Gettysburg Campaign* (2008)

Hess, Earl J., *The Union Soldier in Battle: Enduring the Ordeal of Combat* (1997)

Jimerson, Randall, *The Private Civil War: Popular Thought During the Sectional Conflict* (1988)

McCarter, William (O'Brien, Kevin, ed.) *My Life in the Irish Brigade* (1996)

McPherson, James M., *For Cause and Comrades: Why Men Fought in the Civil War* (1997)

Mitchell, Reid, *Civil War Soldiers: The Expectations and Their Experiences* (1988)

Robertson, James I. Jr., *Soldiers Blue and Gray* (1988)

Sheehan-Dean, Aaron, *The View from the Ground: Experiences of Civil War Soldiers* (2006)

Wiley, Bell I., *The Life of Johnny Reb: The Common Soldier of the Confederacy* (1943)

————, *The Life of Billy Yank: The Common Soldier of the Union* (1952)

African Americans

Berlin, Ira, *Freedom's Soldiers: The Black Military Experience in the Civil War* (1998)

Cornish, Dudley Taylor, *The Sable Arm: Negro Troops in the Union Army, 1861-1865* (1966)

Duncan, Russell, *Where Death and Glory Meet: Robert Gould Shaw and the 54th Massachusetts Infantry* (1999)

Glatthaar, Joseph T., *Forged in Battle: The Civil War Alliance of Black Soldiers and White Officers* (1990)

Higginson, Thomas Wentworth, *Army Life in a Black Regiment, and Other Writings* (1997)

McPherson, James M., *The Negro's Civil War: How American Blacks Felt and Acted During the War for the Union* (1965)

Women

Berlin, Jean V. and Massey, Mary Elizabeth, *Women in the Civil War* (1994)

Clinton, Catherine and Silber, Nina, eds., *Divided Houses: Gender and the Civil War* (1992)

Faust, Drew Gilpin, *Mothers of Invention: Women of the Slaveholding South in the American Civil War* (1996)

Garrison, Nancy S. *With Courage and Delicacy: Civil War on the Peninsula : women and the U.S. Sanitary Commission* (1999)

Leonard, Elizabeth D., *All the Daring of a Soldier: Women of the Civil War Armies* (1999)

Silber, Nina, *Daughters of the Union: Northern Women Fight the Civil War* (2005)

Varon, Elizabeth R., *Southern Lady, Yankee Spy: The True Story of Elizabeth Van Lew, A Union Agent in the Heart of the Confederacy* (2005)

Woodward, C. Vann, ed., *Mary Chestnut's Civil War* (1981)

Native Americans

Confer, Clarissa, *The Cherokee Nation in the Civil War* (2007)

Cunningham, Frank, *General Stand Watie's Confederate Indians* (1959)

Gaines, W. Craig, *The Confederate Cherokees: John Drew's Regiment of Mounted Rifles* (1989)

Grayson, George W., *A Creek Warrior for the Confederacy: The Autobiography of Chief G. W. Grayson* (1991)

Hatch, Thom, *The Blue, the Gray, & the Red: Indian Campaigns of the Civil War* (2001)

Photographic Histories

Frassanito, William A., *Gettysburg: A Journey in Time* (1974)

————, *Antietam: The Photographic Legacy of America's Bloodiest Day* (1978)

Miller, Francis T., ed., *The Photographic History of the Civil War* 10 vols. (1911)

National Historical Society, *Image of War, 1861-1865* 6 vols. (1981-1984)

Time-Life Books, *Civil War Series* 28 vols. (1980s)

Genealogy

Groene, Bertram Hawthorne, *Tracing Your Civil War Ancestor* (1989)

Segars, J. H., *In Search of Confederate Ancestors: The Guide* (1993)

Maps and Cartography

Gottfried, Bradley, *The Maps of Gettysburg: The Gettysburg Campaign, June 3 - July 13, 1863* (2007)

McElfresh, Earl B., *Maps and Mapmakers of the Civil War* (1999)

Miller, William J., *Mapping for Stonewall: The Civil War Service of Jed Hotchkiss* (1993)

National Archives and Records Administration, *Guide to Civil War Maps in the National Archives* (1986)

Nelson, Christopher, and Pohanka, Brian, *Mapping the Civil War: Featuring Rare Maps from the Library of Congress* (1992)

Stephenson, Richard W., comp., *Civil War Maps: An Annotated List of Maps and Atlases in the Library of Congress* (1989)

U.S. War Department, *Atlas to Accompany the Official Records of the Union and Confederate Armies* 2 vols. (1891)

Woodworth, Steven E., and Winkle, Kenneth J. *Atlas of the Civil War* (2004)

Fiction

Crane, Stephen, *The Red Badge of Courage* (1895)

Frazier, Charles, *Cold Mountain* (1997)

Robertston, Don, *The Three Days: A Novel of Gettysburg* (1959)

Shaara, Michael, *The Killer Angels* (1974)

Slotkin, Richard, *The Crater* (1980)

Reference, Documents, and Data

Boatner, Mark M. III, *The Civil War Dictionary* (1959)

Current, Richard N., ed., *Encyclopedia of the Confederacy* 4 vols. (1993)

Dornbusch, C. E., comp, *Military Bibliography of the Civil War* 4 vols. (1971)

Dyer, Frederick Henry, *Compendium of the War of the Rebellion* 2 vols. (1908)

Fox, William F., *Regimental Losses in the American Civil War, 1861-1865* (1889)

Livermore, Thomas L., *Numbers and Losses in the Civil War in America, 1861-65* (1909)

Phisterer, Frederick, *Statistical Record of the Armies of the United States* (1883)

United States Naval War Records Office, *Official Records of the Union and Confederate Navies in the War of the Rebellion* 30 vols. (1894-1922)

United States War Department, *The War of the Rebellion: A Compilation of the Official Records* 129 vols. (1880-1901)

United States Surgeon General's Office, *Medical and Surgical History of the War of the Rebellion, 1861-65* 2 vols. (1870-88)

Warner, Ezra, *Generals in Gray: Lives of the Confederate Commanders* (1959)

————, *Generals in Blue: Lives of the Union Commanders* (1964)

Civil War on the Web

In recent years, the Internet has witnessed an explosion of Web sites dedicated to the Civil War. Some belong to libraries and archives, many of which have shown an interest in making their holdings more accessible to the public. Others are the creations of researchers or enthusiasts who have decided to share their knowledge and findings with a wider audience.

As with all things Internet-related, some sites offer outstanding, quality information, while others push nonsense, quasi-facts, and agendas. The following list aims to point readers to a sampling of reliable and very useful sites. As with all Web sites, the addresses of some may change in the coming years or stop publishing altogether. As of this writing, these sites are all active and thriving.

Libraries and Archives

Library of Congress (www.loc.gov/)

The Web site of the nation's premier repository offers visitors a variety of opportunities for further research. Check out the Digital Collections page (www.loc.gov/library/libarch-digital.html) to search through select manuscript, newspaper, and map collections. For those interested in Civil War images, check out the Prints and Photographs Online Catalog (lcweb2.loc. gov/pp/mdbquery.html).

National Union Catalog of Manuscript Collections (www.loc.gov/coll/nucmc/)

This Library of Congress-maintained site is for the serious researcher. An easy-to-navigate search engine provides visitors with access to descriptions of manuscript collections held by repositories throughout the country. Search for letters, diaries, and other unpublished materials by author's name or regiment, or by subject.

National Archives and Records Administration (www.archives.gov/)

At first blush, the National Archives' site might be a bit intimidating—there are so many options to choose from. Not to worry: start with the Civil War research page (www.archives.gov/research/civil-war/) and go from there.

Minnesota State Archives (www.mnhs.org/)

Those looking for information about their state's role in the war should investigate its archive's Web site. Each of the 50 U.S. state archives maintains a site, and Minnesota's is among the very best when it comes to American Civil War research. www.mnhs.org/collections/civilwar/index.htm offers tips on researching the Civil War through the archive's holdings.

The Brooklyn Public Library (www.brooklynpubliclibrary.org/)

Libraries (large and small) often provide historical information of local interest (sometimes Civil War-related) on their Web sites. Few do so better than the Brooklyn Public Library, whose site devotes an entire section to Brooklyn's role in the conflict (www.brooklynpubliclibrary.org/civilwar/). Included are documents, games, and proposed lesson plans for teachers. Additionally, those interested in reading about the Civil War in real time can do so through the pages of the *Brooklyn Daily Eagle*, the wartime issues of which are available for searching or browsing (eagle.brooklyn publiclibrary.org/)

The Smithsonian (www.si.edu)

Those interested in Civil War artwork and collectibles should not miss the "Civil War @ Smithsonian" page (www.civilwar.si.edu/) produced by the National Portrait Gallery. Collections are broken down into easy-to-browse categories, including "Slavery & Abolition," "Soldiering," "Weapons," and "Life and Culture."

The Army Heritage and Education Center (www.carlisle.army.Mil/ahec/index.htm)

Part of the U.S. Army War College at Carlisle Barracks, Pennsylvania, the Army Heritage and Education Center's site provides access to their comprehensive research holdings. Click on the link for the "MHI Research Catalog" (www.ahco.army.mil/site/index.jsp) to search for Civil War manuscripts, photographs, and artifacts. Of particular interest are the center's Civil War reference bibliographies, which visitors can use to locate the titles and publication information of books and articles written on individual Union and Confederate regiments and armies.

Making of America (cdl.library.cornell.edu/moa/moa_browse.html)

This Cornell University Library site is a boon for Civil War researchers, who are able to search through nineteenth-century editions of a variety of publications, from *Scientific American* to *The Atlantic Monthly*. Of greatest interest are the *Official Records* of the Union and Confederate armies (cdl.library.cornell.edu/moa/moa_browse.html) and navies (cdl.library.Cornell.edu/moa/moa_browse.html).

General Interest

The National Parks Service (www.nps.gov)

Contains a comprehensive list of national parks—including Civil War military sites—throughout the country. Visitors can find information on each park's operating hours and history, obtain a copy of its brochure, and take a virtual tour.

The Civil War Soldiers and Sailors System (www.itd.nps.gov/cwss/)

The National Park Service maintains this site, which contains a searchable database of men who served in the Union and Confederate army and navy. The information comes from the military service records at the National Archives, and includes the soldier's name, rank, and regiment—a good starting point in the search for a Civil War ancestor. Also available are comprehensive battle summaries.

Civil War Preservation Trust (www.civilwar.org/)

This is the official site of the CWPT, whose mission is to protect and preserve battlefield land threatened by modern-day encroachment. There's something for everyone here—from event listings to preservation news to a "History Center" for teachers and students.

The American Civil War Homepage (sunsite.utk.edu/civil-war/warweb.html)

First launched in the mid-1990s, this remarkable site was the product of students in the University of Tennessee's School of Information Sciences. It's grown since then to include links to a massive number of Civil War-related Web pages, broken down into easily searchable categories. From libraries to reenacting units, genealogies to Civil War Round Tables, the ACWH maintains a massive number of links, and updates them regularly. A must-see for researchers is the Civil War Units File, a listing of people (with contact information) willing to share their expertise on particular regiments.

Civil War Interactive (www.civilwarinteractive.com/)

This self-described "Daily Newspaper of the Civil War" offers a variety of interesting and entertaining features, including news stories, book reviews, Civil War recipes, and a discussion board. Don't miss CWI's "LinkCentral," a thorough listing and review of various Civil War Web sites.

Civil War Traveler (www.civilwartraveler.com/)

If you're looking to plan a Civil War-themed trip, then this is the site for you. Event listings, maps, recommended reading, and much more are to be had here, all broken down by region, state, and site.

Antietam on the Web (aotw.org/)

A comprehensive site dedicated to the war's bloodiest single day.

The Historical New York Times Project (www.nyt.ulib.org/)

Search through every issue of the *New York Times* during the Civil War years. Great for researchers, students, and teachers.

Authentic Campaigner (www.authentic-campaigner.com/)

Want to learn about Civil War reenacting? This site—marketed as "A Web Site for the Authentic Civil War Living Historian"—should be first on your list. Lots of information and a vibrant discussion board are its strengths.

The Papers of Jefferson Davis (jeffersondavis.rice.edu/)

This Rice University site is among the best of its kind, and offers visitors a chance to learn about the lone Confederate president through his own writings.

Shotgun's Home of the American Civil War (www.civilwarhome.com/)

Popular with students, this privately run site offers equal doses of information and opinion.

The Naval Historical Center (www.history.navy.mil/)

The official history program of the U.S. Navy maintains this site, which contains an easy-to-search "Research & Collections" section. Visit the "Online Library of Selected Images" (www.history.navy.mil/branches/org11-2.htm) to view images of a wide variety of U.S. and Confederate vessels.

Civil War News (www.civilwarnews.com/)

A monthly newspaper devoted to current events in the Civil War community.

Civil War Book Review (www.cwbr.com/)

A product of Louisiana State University's United States Civil War Center, CWBR contains reviews of the latest Civil War books.

Blogs

Bull Runnings (bullrunnings.wordpress.com/)

A massive and simply outstanding site dedicated to all things related to the First Battle of Bull Run.

Civil War Books & Authors (cwba.blogspot.com/)

A bibliophile's take on Civil War publishing and publications. For anyone interested in new and reprint Civil War titles, this site is indispensable.

Civil War Bookshelf (http://cwbn.blogspot.com/)

An insightful, often colorful, and usually provocative look at Civil War publishing, authors, and historical trends.

Civil War Cavalry (civilwarcavalry.com/)

A historian offers insights into the Civil War's mounted arm and related Civil War news.

Civil War Memory (civilwarmemory.typepad.com/civil_war_memory/)

Maintained by a high school history teacher, this blog is updated regularly and contains a wealth of timely insights on the war and its study.

Civil Warriors (civilwarriors.net/wordpress/)

A group of academic historians write regularly on their profession and research.

Complete Gettysburg Guide (http://www.completegettysburgguide.com)

An outstanding blog / web site by two leading historians on touring Gettysburg and related sites. A must-see site, built around a must-have book.

Gettysburg Daily (Http://www.gettysburgdaily.com)

The *Gettysburg Daily* is an independent website, whose purpose is to provide "at least one picture a day related in some way to Gettysburg." In reality, it is much more than this, and is always worth a look for anyone interested in this always-fascinating battle and campaign.